The *Software*
Sleuth

The *Software*
Sleuth

Martin E. Kaliski

California Polytechnic State University
San Luis Obispo, California

Burton S. Kaliski, Jr.

RSA Data Security
Redwood City, California

WEST PUBLISHING COMPANY

St. Paul ▸ **New York** ▸ **Los Angeles** ▸ **San Francisco**

Copyediting: Sheryl Rose
Text Design: Roslyn Stendahl, Dapper Design
Composition: Carlisle Communications, Ltd.

Library of Congress Cataloging-in-Publication Data

Kaliski, Martin E.
     The software sleuth / Martin E. Kaliski, Burton S. Kaliski, Jr.
          p.   cm.
     Includes bibliographical references and index.
     ISBN 0-314-66810-1 (soft)
     1. Computer software.   I. Kaliski, Burton S.   II. Title.
QA76.754.K34   1991
005-3—dc20   90-46987
                                                     ∞ CIP

This book is dedicated to Raymond Kaliski, 1908–1987, our beloved father and grandfather.

Contents

Examples

Figures

Preface

This is a text about *software sleuthing*—analyzing and understanding computer programs that others have written. That such a skill is useful is clear: In academic and industrial environments alike there are literally thousands of programs that need to be maintained, enhanced, and debugged, and usually this must be done by people who have not written them.

Unfortunately, modern software engineering theory emphasizes how we *ought* to design and write programs, not how people *really* do it. This text attempts to develop some insight into practical methods of software sleuthing.

What kinds of skills must the software sleuth possess?

1. The ability to read programs written by others, very often in older languages such as FORTRAN, COBOL, C, and assembler, and not necessarily in more "modern" languages such as Pascal, Modula-2, and Ada.

2. The ability to enhance, debug, and improve such programs, often without the aid of substantial documentation about either the problem being solved or the algorithms and data structures being used, and often without the assistance of the people who originally developed the programs.

3. The ability to analyze programs with applications in unfamiliar areas.

4. The ability to validate programs, often with limited testing budgets,

limited debugging tools, and limited administrative understanding of the whole concept of software testing.

It is to these capabilities that this book is addressed. We are not specifically concerned here with software engineering theory; such methodology is well covered in many traditional references (see the suggested readings in each chapter for some of these standard references). We are concerned with some very pragmatic "blue collar" issues in the *analysis of existing software,* and are not concerned with the *design* of software except in the context of the maintenance or enhancement of existing programs.

Chapter 1 begins by discussing the environment in which the software sleuth operates. Documentation and organization may be poor. Overly complex algorithms may underlie the programs and the chosen data and control structures may be inefficient. Bugs may exist and the means to fix them may be unknown or at best uncertain. All of these problems manifest themselves in the form of *unreliable,* difficult-to-understand programs.

Chapters 2–6 discuss the primary skills that a software sleuth needs to read programs that someone else has written. We give some common-sense guidelines for addressing this problem, ranging from the obvious (understand the source language and problem domain—Chapter 2) to the subtle (rewrite program documentation, perhaps with the aid of technical writers—Chapter 6). Chapters 3–5 broach the key issues of program modularization, algorithms and data structures, and transcript (test run) analysis. Dealing successfully with all of these areas is the hallmark of the good sleuth. A series of heuristic guidelines to sleuthing is given in these chapters in the form of "Sleuthing Rules."

Throughout the text an example of real-life sleuthing is given, using an "industrial-strength" program written in C. The discussion of this program illustrates the concepts of the material presented in each chapter.

Appendix A describes some common categories of software tools that can be of immense value to the software sleuth. Appendix B consists of the listings of part of the industrial-strength program. Finally, the chapter-by-chapter bibliography lists relevant works in software engineering and programming methodology and other items that may be of interest to the reader.

There are two types of problems at the ends of the various chapters: *exercises,* which deal with specific, concrete examples and issues raised within the text, and *problems,* which delve into more open-ended, less structured issues. A separate instructor's manual accompanies this text, giving solutions to the exercises.

Exercises and examples are closely integrated with the sleuthing guidelines. When they involve actual program fragments, the example programs are written in FORTRAN and C, languages that are commonly sleuthed in industry and academe alike. But the techniques and issues described in the text are language-independent, and comfortably translate into whatever language the sleuth is likely to encounter. Minimal knowledge of MS-DOS directory structures is needed.

This book is written as a stand-alone text, but it can easily be used as a supplementary text in software engineering and software maintenance courses offered at the intermediate to advanced level in computer science programs. Similar courses in other programs such as electrical engineering or industrial engineering could benefit from this text as well. The only background required of the reader is some programming experience and a certain level of mathematical sophistication, a maturity commonly found in upper-division students.

This text draws upon our more than 25 years of practical industrial experience as software sleuths and as teachers of the more academically oriented software engineering methodology. More than anything else, this text is the "memoirs" of two software sleuths.

The authors wish to acknowledge the contributions, direct and indirect, of the following individuals: Peter Wolfe, for showing us how programming should be done; Joe Fisher, Bob Gongloff, and Darwin Dennison, for providing ample opportunities for sleuthing; Karen Lemone, for encouraging the publication of this text; Steve DeRosa, for his critical outlook from the student's perspective; Brian Freeman, for his help with Appendix A; Amr Assal, for his help with the diagrams; and Jim Bidzos, for supporting the final preparation of the text.

We also thank the following reviewers for their constructive criticism:

Kevin Bowyer
University of South Florida

James E. Burns
Georgia Institute of Technology

R. H. Campbell
University of Illinois at
Urbana-Champaign

Paul Grabow
University of Texas at Arlington

Sallie Henry
Virginia Tech

Stephen P. Hufnagel
University of Texas at Arlington

Ann Miller
University of New Mexico

Robert G. Reynolds
Wayne State University

Walter Scacchi
University of Southern California

Joseph L. Zachary
University of Utah

Special thanks to Mike Slaughter of West Educational Publishing, who helped guide this project to its completion.

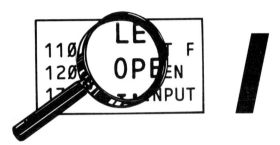

Software Sleuthing: Demystifying the Software Maintenance Process

The theme of this book has its origins in the following anecdote. You begin work one fine day for the XYZ Technology Company. Your manager welcomes you with a version of the following woeful tale:

Our best applications programmer quit last week, after having been with the firm for over seven years. We are a small firm, and she was not only our best programmer, but often our only one. All the programs she wrote were in (fill in your favorite language), and they all pretty much functioned as required. That's the good news. The bad news is that when it came to documentation, we never had the time to do it right, and she wasn't so inclined anyway. The fact is no one else has even looked at over half of this code, and she's about the only one who understands what it really does.

Our problem now is that our new client, ABC Applications, Ltd., wants us to enhance this software to run on their specialized equipment. Our star programmer of the past is unavailable for *any* help at this point. Now, we have the support staff here to install the software on the new equipment and even to write the upgrades needed, but we do not have anyone who has the time, interest, or skill to first figure out what's here right now. Your job, in brief, is to document what has been done, explain it, tell us if it works and how it works, and what bugs, if any, are present. In other words, you are to be our *software sleuth.*

What do you do? (Quitting is *not* an option.) How do you even begin to tackle a problem such as this?

This is an all too common situation in both industry and academe. It is a problem without clear-cut solutions. Understand that the sleuth cannot simply sit down and read the software line-by-line at the start of his or her detective work, although ultimately such "linear" reading will have to be done. This is seldom viable, since programs are usually not written linearly. The sleuth must find an approach that has at least a reasonable chance of unraveling the existing nest of programs.

Typical among the problems faced by the sleuth are the following:

▶ inadequate documentation and program specification

▶ poor organization of the program modules

▶ overly complex algorithms within the modules

▶ overly complex data structures within the modules

▶ inadequate program testing and test results

In the chapters that follow we will discuss these and other problems as we develop a practical approach for sleuthing already-written programs. We will develop sleuthing guidelines, or "Rules," and will reinforce our discussions with a case study of a rather large program written in C—a real-life example of "industrial-strength" sleuthing.

First, we present a few examples that typify the environment the sleuth often finds himself or herself in. We then give a road map for the remainder of the text and say a few words about our industrial-strength example.

1.1 The Sleuthing Environment: Some Examples

The list of examples below is by no means complete. View it as the appetizer for the full-course meal that follows in the remainder of the text.

Example 1–1

But the Code Is Self-Documenting

The year was 1974, but the story is timeless. Only the language and application may differ from one version to another. PL/I is a Pascal-like, block-structured language, for those readers not familiar with it.

One of the authors once had a colleague who steadfastly refused to write *any* accompanying documentation for his PL/I programs. He claimed that his programs were replete with comments and that PL/I, being a highly readable, block-structured language, was *self-documenting*. He said, in fact, that "the best documentation for what the code is doing is the code itself." He went on to say (almost in complete reversal of modern software engineering methodology) that because of the nature of the programming language used, it was redundant to be concerned with such issues as program specifications or requirements.

When called upon by contractual commitments to add documentation to his programs, he begrudgingly invoked an automatic flowchart-creation utility that worked from the source program to produce flowcharts for it. He was right in a way—these proved to be rather useless. His flowcharts and other documentation aids should have been developed *before and concurrent with* program writing, and not *afterwards*.

Experience confirms the sad fact that much of the early work done by the software sleuth involves filling in missing pieces of documentation. This is often akin to doing a jigsaw puzzle without a complete picture of what it is supposed to look like.

(Oh, as for the ending of the story, it was not at all unexpected. The flowcharts were delivered and no one read them. The project, alas, ran out of funding and the programs died a slow, undocumented death.)

Example 1-2

Isn't This a Terrible Novel?

In many ways, a program is like a novel. It has a beginning and an end and a kind of narrative. Each action in a program is a subplot of sorts; each decision branches to alternative scenarios in the narrative. The things that make a novel hard to read often make a program hard to read as well. Software sleuths are in some ways literary critics and do not rate hard-to-read books or hard-to-read programs among their favorites.

What kinds of things make books hard to read?

▶ subject matter that is intrinsically difficult

▶ poor use of language, or use of a foreign language

▶ poor choice of names for characters

▶ poor organization and division into chapters

▶ relationships between events that are overly subtle or complex (e.g., flashbacks, dream sequences)

▶ excessive length for the subject at hand

If one thinks in terms of the software environment, the same issues arise. The application area of the program is akin to the subject matter of a book. The source language of a program is akin to the language of the book, with different language features reflecting different writing styles. If an algorithm is written in a language that is well known and easy to follow, the program should be relatively easy to read. If it is in a language known by just a small portion of the general population, then—all other things being equal—the program is probably more difficult to read. Such difficulties increase the time it takes the sleuth to come up to speed on the language and to make changes or enhancements. Certain special situations may require a difficult language or writing style, but these are usually the exception, not the rule.

Similarly, if programmers often choose meaningless and overly vague names for variables (e.g., "TABLE2," "MARSHA," "tiger"), as opposed to names that convey something about the role of the variable in the overall scheme of things (e.g., "TEMP_COEFF," "offset_tab2"), then understanding the program is more difficult. When numerical labels in a language like FORTRAN appear in a sequence that seems completely arbitrary, as opposed to having *some* logical order, it is very hard to find statements in the program. Would you buy a book in which the page numbers and cross-references were completely arbitrary? Issues such as these require great patience on the part of the sleuth.

Example 1–3

The Fancy Programmer

The software sleuth is very often confronted with unexplained or overly complex algorithms. Suppose, for example, that the purpose of a program is to compute the integer square root IROOT(N) of a positive integer N, i.e., the largest integer whose square is less than or equal to N. Thus IROOT(11) = 3, IROOT(25) = 5, and IROOT(103) = 10. The straightforward way of doing this is to walk through a loop, squaring in turn $1, 2, \ldots, j, \ldots$ until j^2 exceeds N. The desired square root is then $j-1$.

In pseudocode the above algorithm is concisely expressed as:

$$j \leftarrow 1$$
$$\textbf{while } j^2 \leq N$$
$$\quad \textbf{do } j \leftarrow j + 1$$
$$\textbf{return } j-1$$

Suppose, however, that the programmer chose to implement it in the following "fancy" way, without any accompanying documentation. Pseudocode is again used to illustrate this "overly complex" algorithm:

$$j \leftarrow 1$$
$$k \leftarrow 1$$
$$\textbf{while } k \leq N$$
$$\quad \textbf{do } j \leftarrow j + 1$$
$$\qquad k \leftarrow k + 2j - 1$$
$$\textbf{return } j-1$$

Sleuths see this kind of thing all the time. Unless the original programmer indicated somewhere that the sum of the first M odd numbers is M^2 (right?), the sleuth would need to deduce the fact himself or herself—an expenditure that could have been avoided with a single comment.

There are, to be sure, situations in which the more straightforward algorithm for doing something is less efficient, in terms of either execution time or storage use. Is this the case with the above example? If the reader concludes it is (see the Exercises), then taking such a circuitous approach to finding the integer square root of N may be justified—and some comments should explain the reasons why it has been so implemented.

All too often, however, there is no apparent justification for overly complex algorithms, and the software sleuth is, unfortunately, left with the nagging suspicion that he or she has missed something important.

1.2 A Road Map for the Remainder of the Text

In Chapter 2, we discuss an admittedly obvious pair of preliminary steps that the sleuth must take before he or she can make any real progress. The first we term "know the language." This does not mean memorizing the language reference manual. It means learning or reviewing the salient features of the language to eliminate as much of the "language barrier" as possible. We also discuss the importance of appreciating the choice of source language. The second step is equally intuitive. The sleuth must "know the application" area of the program.

In Chapter 3, we address the need for the sleuth to understand the modular structure of the program. In Chapter 4 we turn to the modules themselves and the need to identify key data and control structures within them.

Chapter 5 turns to the study of existing transcripts (test runs) of the program and to the need for creating new transcripts to refine and validate a mental model of the program.

Chapter 6 turns to documentation—putting into words the stable model achieved when the sleuth finally understands the program. Two essential types of documentation are described.

Each chapter illustrates the corresponding phase of sleuthing just discussed in the context of an industrial-strength example: "The Case of the DINE ® Statistics/Graphics Program." The Statistics/Graphics Program implements algorithms for collecting and displaying statistics on the nutritional behavior of individuals and groups.*

We suggest at this point that you mentally prepare yourself for this "case" by quickly thumbing through the listings in Appendix B. You will see a large number of procedures in C. The goal of the sleuthing process, of course, is to figure out what this program does and somehow to tell the world about it.

The entire process of software sleuthing is intrinsically *incremental*, for often one is concerned with understanding only a portion of a much larger whole. Although we have posed the problem of understanding the "entire" program, the methodology introduced in this text can be used to understand only a portion of a program *provided* the portion is truly self-contained.

Be aware that we are espousing *general principles* for understanding a program. The principles will, of course, vary in importance, depending upon the specific program being sleuthed.

---

*The Statistics/Graphics Program is a product of DineSystems Inc., Buffalo, NY, © 1988 Dr. Darwin Dennison, and is sleuthed with Dr. Dennison's permission.

1.3 Conventions

The text makes numerous references to procedures, variables, and files in the Statistics/Graphics Program. Procedures and variables are indicated in a computer typeface (e.g., "the procedure `menu_3`," "the variable `record`"); files are written in that typeface in uppercase and contain the .C or .H extension (e.g., "the file `MENU_003.C`"). The names of all of the procedures and variables referenced in the text are included in the index.

▶▶▶▶▶ *Exercises*

1–1. Draw a flowchart or write pseudocode for the following uncommented FORTRAN program fragment and try to state "abstractly" what it does. What data structures are assumed? (Now you know how a sleuth makes a living.)

```
        DO 10 I = 1,N
        IF (I.GT.1) GOTO 11
        A = X(I)
        B = A
        C = A
        GOTO 10
  11    IF (X(I).LT.A) A = X(I)
        IF (X(I).GT.B) B = X(I)
        C = C+X(I)
  10    CONTINUE
```

1–2. Repeat Exercise 1–1 for the following fragment. How might you improve this program fragment?

```
        I1 = 1
        I2 = 1
        J = 1
  10    IF (I1.GT.N1) GOTO 12
        IF (I2.GT.N2) GOTO 11
        IF (X1(I1).GT.X2(I2)) GOTO 12
  11    IF (I1.GT.N1) GOTO 14
        Y(J) = X1(I1)
        I1 = I1+1
        GOTO 13
  12    IF (I2.GT.N2) GOTO 14
        Y(J) = X2(I2)
        I2 = I2+1
  13    J = J+1
        GOTO 10
  14    CONTINUE
```

1–3. Repeat Exercise 1–1 for the following fragment:

```
        I = 1
        J = 1
10      IF (I.GT.N) GOTO 13
        IF (X(I).NE.9) GOTO 12
        DO 11 J1 = J,(J+7)/8*8
        Y(J1) = 32
11      CONTINUE
        J = J1+1
        I = I+1
        GOTO 10
12      Y(J) = X(I)
        J = J+1
        I = I+1
        GOTO 10
13      CONTINUE
```

1–4. Repeat Exercise 1–1 for the following fragment:

```
        W = EXP(CMPLX(0.0,-2*PI/N))
        WK = (1.0,0.0)
        DO 10 K = 1,N
        F(K) = (0.0,0.0)
        WKI = (1.0,0.0)
        DO 20 I = 1,N
        F(K) = F(K)+T(I)*WKI
        WKI = WKI*WK
20      CONTINUE
        WK = WK*W
10      CONTINUE
```

1–5. Consider the two square root programs presented in Example 1–3. If multiplication and addition take the same amount of time, which square root program is faster? Is there a good reason to choose the more complex program or not?

1–6. Consider the following "transcript" of the output of the C program below that simulates the movement of an object up, down, left, and right, one unit at a time, in an integer grid (user input is shown in boldface):

```
Postion (0, 0).
Action: U

Position (0, 0).
Action: D

Position (0, -1).
Action: L
```

```
Position (0, -1).
Action: R

Position (1, -1).
Action:
```

a. The program has two errors. Examine the transcript to determine them.

b. Now examine the program itself, and state and correct the errors.

```
main () {
    int x = 0, y = 0;
    char c;

    while (1) {
      printf ("\nPosition    (%d, %d).\n", x, y);
      printf ("Action: ");
      scanf ("%c", &c);
      switch (c) {
          case 'U': y++;
          case 'D': y--;
          case 'L': x--;
          case 'R': x++;
      }
    }
}
```

In this problem the sleuth is using program output to gain clues about program behavior.

1–7. The following function written in C has considerable inefficiencies and is overly complex. Describe the operation of the function, find the inefficiencies, and suggest an improvement. This is sleuthing at its most fun.

```
int member (int x[], int n, int e)
{
  if (n <= 0) return (0);
  if (n == 1) return (x[0] == e);
  return (member (&x[0], n/2, e) ||
          member (&x[n/2], n-(n/2), e));
}
```

1–8. Repeat Exercise 1–7 for the following subroutine written in FORTRAN:

```
      SUBROUTINE TRANSP(X,N)
      REAL X(N,N),Y(100,100)
C
      IF (N.GT.100) RETURN
```

```
C
      DO 10 I = 1,N
      DO 10 J = 1,N
      Y(J,I) = X(I,J)
10    CONTINUE
C
      DO 20 I = 1,N
      DO 20 J = 1,N
      X(I,J) = Y(I,J)
20    CONTINUE
      RETURN
      END
```

►►►►► *Problems*

1-1. Add to the list of sleuthing problems discussed in this chapter by calling upon your own experiences with other people's programs.

1-2. Choose several software packages with which you are familiar. Become a "documentation critic" and judge how well they are documented. Look at both commercial and noncommercial packages.

1-3. Using the "literary analogy model" of Example 1-2, evaluate the organization and style of several books you have read recently. Now apply these criteria to evaluate several programs you have used or written lately. Is this analogy really a good one for *you?*

1-4. Look over a few of the recent programs you have written. Estimate the number of different possible input combinations on which they could conceivably be run. How many such cases have you actually tested them on? Does this make you feel very confident about their correctness?

1-5. A common problem in software engineering is keeping documentation up to date in the presence of continually evolving programs. This is the so-called "moving target syndrome." Identify the kinds of problems that are likely to arise in this environment, despite one's best intentions and self-discipline.

1-6. One language feature that is often extended beyond the language standard is input/output. If you have the documentation available, compare the standard set of I/O features for a particular language with the set defined for that language on a *particular* computer system. Discuss the differences. Proportionately, what fraction of the I/O features defined for the system are not standard? What advantage does this have for programs written for the system? What disadvantages? Why must the sleuth be aware of these issues?

1–7. Repeat Problem 1–6 for the following language features:

a. control structures

b. built-in data types

c. intrinsic functions

1–8. Problems 1–6 and 1–7 considered the differences between the standard features of a language and the features defined for a particular computer system. Now consider, if you have the documentation available, the differences between the language "dialects" defined for two different computer systems. All standard features should be the same for both systems, but extensions may or may not be. Moreover, extensions may have the same syntax but different meanings, which may make the program ambiguous to the software sleuth. If you have the documentation available, list the language extensions defined for the two systems, indicating whether each extension is

a. defined for only one system, being syntactically incorrect for the other

b. defined for both systems and having the same meaning

c. defined for both systems and having a different meaning for each

In the third case, indicate how the ambiguity of the extension might affect the software sleuth's ability to understand a program.

Suggested Readings

Modern software engineering finds many of its roots in the "software crisis" of the 1970s. Concerning this crisis E. W. Dijkstra observed in his Turing-award article (1972): "Now that we have gigantic computers, programming has become an equally gigantic problem." In the last five years the importance of software engineering has become increasingly clear. Britcher and Craig's article in *IEEE Software* (1986) describes an effort to modernize the aging FAA air traffic control system in which software engineering principles played a key role. A good overview of the problems and future of software engineering can be found in Ramamoorthy, Prakash, Tsai, and Usuda (1984).

Software sleuthing has also come into view lately in the topics of design recovery and software evolution. An example of the kinds of systems that may become the tools of the future for software sleuths is the Desire system, which "helps software engineers understand programs by analyzing code, relying on the analyst's own reasoning, and drawing on a knowledge base of design expectations" (Biggerstaff 1989).

To the sleuth who wants to write programs that need less sleuthing, we recommend such reading as Brooks's classic on the design of the IBM

360 (1975), Bentley's pearls (1986, 1988) and Ledgard's proverbs (1975), and Kernighan and Plauger's elements of style (1978).

There are a number of good textbooks in software engineering and programming methodology. Two nice, thorough textbooks are Sommerville's (1985) and Fairley's (1985), with Pressman's serving as an additional reference (1988). For object-oriented programming, Cox's (1986) is worthwhile reading. A nice complement to the other books is Deutsch and Willis's (1988), which focuses on management issues.

Some books focus on particular languages: Liskov and Guttag's (1986) teaches data abstraction in the programming language CLU, and Pomberger's (1986) teaches software engineering in Modula-2. Myers's treatise (1978) is a very readable handbook on how to modularize medium and large programs. Shooman (1983) approaches software engineering from reliability theory, giving broad coverage. Our analogy between programs and literature is adapted from Shooman's text. Jackson (1983) gives a unique approach to design. For a mathematical foundation, we recommend Gries's book (1981).

References

Bentley, Jon. *Programming Pearls*. New York: Association for Computing Machinery, 1986.

Bentley, Jon. *More Programming Pearls: Confessions of a Coder*. New York: Association for Computing Machinery, 1988.

Biggerstaff, Ted J. Design recovery for maintenance and reuse. *Computer* 22:36–49, July 1989.

Britcher, Robert N., and James J. Craig. Using modern design practices to upgrade aging software systems. *IEEE Software* 3:16–26, May 1986.

Brooks, F. P., Jr. *The Mythical Man-Month: Essays on Software Engineering*. Reading, MA: Addison-Wesley, 1975.

Cox, B. J. *Object-Oriented Programming: An Evolutionary Approach*. Reading, MA: Addison-Wesley, 1986.

Deutsch, Michael S., and Ronald R. Willis. *Software Quality Engineering: A Total Technical and Management Approach*. Englewood Cliffs, NJ: Prentice-Hall, 1988.

Dijkstra, Edsger W. The humble programmer. *Communications of the ACM* 15:859–886, October 1972.

Fairley, Richard E. *Software Engineering Concepts*. New York: McGraw-Hill, 1985.

Gries, D. *The Science of Programming*. New York: Springer-Verlag, 1981.

Jackson, M. *System Development*. Englewood Cliffs, NJ: Prentice-Hall, 1983.

Kernighan, B. W., and P. J. Plauger. *The Elements of Programming Style*. New York: McGraw-Hill, 1978.

Ledgard, Henry. *Programming Proverbs and Principles*. Rochelle Park, NJ: Hayden, 1975.

Liskov, Barbara, and John Guttag. *Abstraction and Specification in Program Development.* Cambridge, MA: MIT Press, 1986.

Myers, G. J. *Composite/Structured Design.* New York: Van Nostrand-Reinhold, 1978.

Pomberger, Gustav. *Software Engineering and Modula-2.* Englewood Cliffs, NJ: Prentice-Hall, 1986.

Pressman, Roger S. *Making Software Engineering Happen: A Guide for Instituting the Technology.* Englewood Cliffs, NJ: Prentice-Hall, 1988.

Ramamoorthy, C. V., Atul Prakash, Wei-Tek Tsai, and Yutaka Usuda. Software engineering: Problems and perspectives. *Computer* 17:191–209, October 1984.

Sommerville, Ian. *Software Engineering.* 2d ed. Reading, MA: Addison-Wesley, 1985.

Shooman, M. L. *Software Engineering: Reliability, Development, and Management.* New York: McGraw-Hill, 1983.

2

Deciphering the Code: Exploiting Knowledge of Programming Language and Problem Domain

In this chapter we look at the first of our sets of sleuthing guidelines. These concern obtaining knowledge about both the language or languages used in implementing the software and the problem domain involved.

In Section 2.1 we discuss the general issue of language in the context of sleuthing. In Section 2.2 we delve briefly into the more general issue of appreciating the choice of programming language and what this choice may suggest about the nature of the algorithms and data structures in the program. In Section 2.3 we turn to a discussion of the program problem domain. Each section ends with a summary "rule," which is illustrated for the Statistics/Graphics Program. A concluding section and exercises and problems follow.

2.1 Knowing the Language

Most sleuths are not programming language experts. Either they are totally unfamiliar with a given programming language, i.e., have never programmed in it, or they have mastered only a subset of the language in question, a subset that meets their everyday needs. Even sleuths who have programmed for years in such common languages as FORTRAN or Pascal usually only have expertise in a core portion of those languages. The sleuths simply do not need or, more likely, do not use the other features of the language.

The implication of this lack of expertise is that it never hurts the sleuth to browse through a programming language reference as an initial sleuthing step. After all, it could be that the original programmers preferred a somewhat different subset of the language than the one the sleuth knows well. Certainly if the sleuth is called upon to study programs written in an unfamiliar language he or she must study the language manual, but even if the language is familiar, review and reassimilation is important. Review may suggest long-forgotten features or even new ways of approaching a given program—e.g., "I didn't realize that one could do an IF-THEN-ELSE in FORTRAN." Review will also make the sleuth aware of library procedures for certain basic functions.

The "rehashing" process is, by nature, an iterative one. We never try to read a manual from cover to cover—it is too boring for most people and much too detailed. We skim, reskim, go back to the program, repeat the process, and so on.

We make a final note. If a program contains machine-dependent I/O features, or is partially written in assembly language or micro-code, then some time must be spent in becoming familiar with the machine's architecture. It is artificial to make a separation between software and hardware; in the real world this often cannot and should not be done.

Example 2–1

A Sorting Program and its Language

You are given the FORTRAN program MINSORT shown in Figure 2–1. As a first step, which features of FORTRAN might you need to be familiar with? Consider the following questions. If you are not familiar with this material, now is a good time to become so. Answers are given below.

1. How are arguments passed?

2. What is the meaning of the statement "DO 1000 I = 1, N-1"?

3. What is the meaning of the statement "ACCEPT *, N, (A(K), K = 1,N)"?

4. Some variables (e.g., N in MINSORT) are not declared explicitly. What are their data types?

Answers:

1. Call by reference. The arguments' addresses are passed to the subroutine. Changes to an argument in the subroutine are thus visible to the calling procedure.

2. Repeat the block of statements between the "DO" statement and label "1000" for the variable I taking the values 1, 2, . . . , N − 1. (We overlook many subtleties.)

3. The "ACCEPT *" statement performs free-format input from the terminal. The first value read is stored in N; the next N values read are stored in A(1), . . . , A(N), respectively, according to what is termed an "implied DO-loop."

4. In general, the data type of a variable not declared explicitly is determined by the "I-N" rule. If the variable name begins with the letter *I, J, K, L, M,* or *N,* its data type is INTEGER. Otherwise its data type is REAL.

▶ **Figure 2–1   MINSORT Program**

```
      PROGRAM MINSORT
      INTEGER A(100)
C
      CALL INPUT(A, N)
      CALL SORT(A, N)
      CALL OUTPUT(A, N)
      STOP
      END
C
C     INPUT module -----------------------------------
C
      SUBROUTINE INPUT(A, N)
      INTEGER A(100)
C
      TYPE *, 'please enter list to be sorted'
      TYPE *, 'enter length of list, then list'
      ACCEPT *, N, (A(K), K = 1, N)
      TYPE *, 'original list is ', (A(K), K = 1, N)
      RETURN
      END
C
C     SORT module ------------------------------------
C
      SUBROUTINE SORT(A, N)
      INTEGER A(100), PLACE
C
      DO 1000 I = 1, N-1
C
      MIN = A(I)
      PLACE = I
C
      DO 500 J = I+1, N
C
      IF(A(J) .LT. MIN) THEN
           PLACE = J
           MIN = A(J)
      ENDIF
C
```

```
500     CONTINUE
C
        CALL SWAP(A(I), A(PLACE))
C
1000    CONTINUE
        RETURN
        END
C
C       SWAP module ------------------------------
C
        SUBROUTINE SWAP(X, Y)
        INTEGER X, Y, TEMP
C
        TEMP = X
        X = Y
        Y = TEMP
C
        RETURN
        END
C
C       OUTPUT module ----------------------------
C
        SUBROUTINE OUTPUT(A, N)
        INTEGER A(100)
C
        TYPE *, 'sorted list is', (A(K), K = 1, N)
        RETURN
        END
```

Example 2–2

The Statistics/Graphics Program's Language

Consider the Statistics/Graphics Program. You learn that the program is written primarily in Microsoft C 5.0 for the IBM PC running MS-DOS. (Some of its low-level graphics routines—not listed in Appendix B—are written in assembly language.) In addition to becoming familiar with such IBM PC and MS-DOS features as the graphics interface, the keyboard interface, and the file hierarchy, you would need to understand the Microsoft C run-time library, a graphics library, and certain nonstandard features of Microsoft C 5.0. (When we say "nonstandard" we mean not Kernighan and Ritchie (1978) C. "ANSI standard" C is described in Kernighan and Ritchie (1988).)

We now discuss some of the observations you might make.

Function Declarations

One of the nonstandard features concerns function declarations and headers. In Kernighan and Ritchie C, the data types of dummy arguments to a function are declared outside the argument list, as, for example, in the Statistics/Graphics Program's procedure main:

```
main (argc,argv)
int argc;
char *argv[];
```

Microsoft C 5.0 also supports the ANSI-standard syntax in which the data types are declared inside the argument list, as in the following alternative to `main`:

```
main (int argc, char *argv[])
```

The Statistics/Graphics Program employs both syntaxes.

Variable-Length Argument Lists

Microsoft C 5.0 allows a function to have a list of arguments whose length is not determined until run time. Such a list is indicated with the special variable name `va_alist` and the special data type `va_dcl`. The procedure `message` is an example:

```
message(option,va_alist)
int option;
va_dcl
```

Some parts of the program denote the variable-length part of the list with an ellipsis (. . .).

Void Data Types

The data type `void` indicates either an empty argument list or a function with no return value. No variable ever has this data type. An example is the procedure `show_cursor`:

```
void show_cursor(void)
```

Static Functions

One other feature of C that is of note is the meaning of `static` when applied to functions: A static function is visible only within the file in which it is defined. Thus two or more static functions in different files can have the same name. The Statistics/Graphics Program has several examples of static functions. One example is the procedure `modify` in the file `MENU_006.C`. Note that `modify` in the file `MENU_003.C` is *not* static.

SLEUTHING RULE I

As seen from Examples 2–1 and 2–2, as a first step in reading any program written by someone else, we should adhere to the following rule of software sleuthing: Know the language. Familiarize yourself with the language of the program and any standard library procedures.

2.2 *Appreciating the Choice of Source Language*

During the course of a sleuth's career, he or she is likely to encounter many different programming languages, both procedural and object-oriented, both high-level and low-level. It is important that any existing preferences or distastes for certain languages not interfere with the sleuthing process. So it is useful for the sleuth to have an understanding of the issues that dictate language choice. After all, the best detectives in popular novels succeed by trying to understand the mentality of the criminals they are pursuing.

Very often, language choices are imposed by constraints largely external to the application or computing environment at hand. We return to this in a moment.

If language choice *is* correlated to computing issues, often there is an attempt by the programmer to match a language's capabilities to the problem being solved. If a problem basically involves arithmetic or trigonometric computation and one-, two-, or three-dimensional linear arrays, then it is not surprising to find that the program is written in FORTRAN. If the problem involves communicating with I/O ports, memories, and communications buses, then assembly language or C may be used. If recursive and other specialized structures are required, then a more sophisticated language is called for, perhaps an object-oriented language such as Modula-2 or C++. Thus the language the program is written in often tells the sleuth something about the nature of the problem being solved.

As for external constraints forcing language choice, an anecdote will suffice to explain the problem. The sleuth should try to understand if such constraints are present. One of the authors recalls an intense argument between two of his colleagues along the following lines. The year was 1974, when PL/I was "the" modern language. (This anecdote involves the same personnel as in Example 1–1. Colleague 2 below was the boss.)

Colleague 1:

The best language—in fact the only language—to use for this industrial automation problem is LISP. Any fool can see that. This is an expert system and the data structures and algorithms demand it.

Colleague 2:

The industry we are dealing with is traditional. They have never heard of LISP. They speak FORTRAN. If we give them something in LISP, they will have great difficulty understanding it, let alone enhancing it. They will view us as pompous intellectuals.

Colleague 1:

I will not write programs in FORTRAN. You're insulting me by even suggesting it.

Colleague 2:

Do you like your job?

Colleague 1:

Will you settle for PL/I?

Colleague 2:

Yes.

It turned out that even PL/I was a bad choice, for the FORTRAN mentality of the industry involved was too deeply ingrained. The point is, nontechnical issues often affect the choice of language. The truly successful software sleuth pays heed to these issues.

Example 2-3

The Choice of the Language C for the Statistics/Graphics Program

The Statistics/Graphics Program is written in C except for some graphics procedures. How does awareness of this choice of language help the sleuth? To begin with, it suggests that the programmers probably were interested in efficiency more than "safety," since C allows much more "dangerous" freedom in operating on memory than do other languages. It also suggests that data structures play an important role in the program. The sleuth should deal with this language choice then by cataloging data structures, looking for unsafe operations, and expecting to unravel some efficient but complex program fragments.

SLEUTHING RULE 2

Summarizing, we have our second rule: Appreciate the choice of source language. The answer to the question "Why was this particular language chosen?" may provide insight into the nature of the algorithms and the programming style.

2.3 Understanding the Application

The authors are not signal processing specialists. Nonetheless, we were once called upon to sleuth some software that implemented various advanced signal processing algorithms. This is not an uncommon situation. No one can be an expert in all fields. The software sleuth must learn enough about an applications area to complete his or her study. We did not have to understand fully the theory underlying the signal processing algorithms. But we did need to recognize that they expected inputs in certain forms, implemented certain recurrences, and produced outputs in certain forms—and that was all we needed to know.

We note that if a program is modularized well (we discuss modularization further in Chapter 3), the sleuth may be able to understand many procedures without knowing the application. An example of good modularization is one that separates application-dependent modules from application-independent modules such as data manipulation and I/O. In such programs the sleuth can study the application-independent modules with a minimum of application expertise.

The point is this: the experienced software sleuth allocates time to become "conversational" in the application, to talk to experts, and to learn, more than anything, to accept certain operations on "faith." In brief, he or she must know the intended audience.

Example 2–4

A Chemistry Program

You are given the FORTRAN program ORBIT shown in Figure 2–2. You are told that it is software written for chemists and has something to do with atoms, electrons, and so on. From the program alone, you determine the following facts.

1. ORBIT inputs an integer and outputs one or more strings of the form "$a\,X\,b$", where a and b are integers and X is one of the letters "S," "P," "D," and "F."

2. The output strings are determined by repeatedly subtracting a quantity 4*L+2 from the input. If the remaining value Y is larger than 4*L+2, the integer b in the output is 4*L+2; otherwise, b is set to Y and output stops.

3. The pairs (NL,L) follow a sequence that begins

$$(1,0),$$
$$(2,0),$$
$$(3,1),\ (3,0),$$
$$(4,1),\ (4,0),$$
$$(5,2),\ (5,1),\ (5,0),$$
$$(6,2),\ (6,1),\ (6,0)$$

The purpose of the sequence is not apparent.
To really understand ORBIT, you need to consult a chemistry text (the suggested readings list some) to find the following facts:

▶ An atom of an element with atomic number Z has Z electrons.

▶ Electrons are organized according to a principal quantum number N which is at least 1 and a subsidiary quantum number L which is at least 0 and at most $N-1$.

▶ In each atom at most $4L+2$ electrons have a given pair (N,L) of principal and subsidiary quantum numbers.

▶ As a general rule, atoms are built up from electrons in increasing order of $N+L$, and among those with the same $N+L$, in increasing order of N. (Chemists know many exceptions to this rule, of course.) Put another way, pairs are assigned as follows:

$$(1,0),$$
$$(2,0),$$
$$(2,1), (3,0),$$
$$(3,1), (4,0),$$
$$(3,2), (4,1), (5,0),$$
$$(4,2), (5,1), (6,0)$$

This bears a striking resemblance to the pairs (NL,L) in ORBIT, which should lead the sleuth to conclude that NL is meant to be the sum $N+L$ and the program is showing how the atom with atomic number Z is built up from electrons.

▶ **Figure 2–2 ORBIT Program**

```
       PROGRAM ORBIT
       INTEGER Z, Y
       INTEGER SO(4)
       DATA SO /'S', 'P', 'D', 'F'/
C
1      ACCEPT *, Z
       Y = Z
C
       DO 10 NL = 1, 8
          DO 11 L = (NL-1)/2, 0, -1
             IF (Y .GT. 4*L+2) GOTO 12
                TYPE 90, NL-L, SO(L+1), Y
                GOTO 20
12              TYPE 90, NL-L, SO(L+1), 4*L+2
                Y = Y - (4*L+2)
11        CONTINUE
10     CONTINUE
C
20     GOTO 1
C
90     FORMAT(1X, I1, A1, I2)
       END
```

Example 2–5

The Statistics/Graphics Program's Application Area

The purpose of the Statistics/Graphics Program is to collect statistics on the nutritional behavior of individuals and groups, to analyze those statistics, and to display the results of that analysis graphically. When we began sleuthing this program we were able to determine its purpose from preliminary requirements documents, some preliminary user documentation, and the program itself. We also benefited from several discussions with the staff of the company that produced the program, though not with the original programmers.

Our examination and discussions revealed that the program was primarily menu-driven and function key–driven and that its central feature was a spreadsheet in which a user could enter a list of nutritional data files. The analysis consisted of comparing the values of any of the several variables stored in those data files. One could compare values over time, against one another, among groups of individuals, or with respect to a particular point in time. The point in time in the latter type of comparison would often be the time of an "intervention"—a change in diet, for example. Nutritionists were the primary market for the program.

We also learned that the files containing data on nutritional behavior were generated by another program, The DINE System, and that those files were in one of two formats. We reasoned, consequently, that we could learn much about the Statistics/Graphics Program from examining The DINE System and its documentation. (We have not included source programs or documentation for The DINE System in this text.)

Our preliminary study of the Statistics/Graphics Program gave us a mental model of the behavior of the program sufficient to ask four questions:

1. How are data files selected in the spreadsheet and what other items can be entered?

2. What are the various menus and function keys and how are they related?

3. How are data stored internally?

4. What are the possible graphs and statistics?

We return to the first three questions in subsequent chapters as we consider the clues that the sleuth might uncover in search of answers. The fourth we address next.

Example 2–6

The Statistics/Graphics Program's Statistics

Let us address the question "What are the possible graphs and statistics?" by looking at the file STATS.C. We answer this question here for possible statistics and leave the other part for the exercises in Chapter 4.

The file STATS.C contains six procedures, three of which compute statistics. Rather than attempt to determine when or why the three statistical procedures are called, we simply sleuth them in isolation. We are able to do this because the specification of the procedures is at least partially defined by the statistics themselves. In Chapter 4 we will discuss in more detail how to sleuth algorithms; here we focus on knowing the application.

Let us look at one procedure, Spearman. (Exercise 2–7 looks at Kruskal_Wallis and Wilcoxon.) The comment in STATS.C (coupled with a standard statistics textbook) tells us that Spearman *should* do the following to N pairs of data $(x_1, y_1), \ldots, (x_N, y_N)$.

1. Rank the x and y parts: Assign integers $\text{rank}_x(i)$ and $\text{rank}_y(i)$ between 1 and N such that x_i is the $\text{rank}_x(i)$-th least element among the x parts and y_i is the

rank$_y(i)$-th least element among the y parts. (Ties are handled differently.)

2. Calculate differences of ranks, $d(i) = rank_x(i) - rank_y(i)$.

3. Return the value

$$1 - \frac{6(d(1)^2 + \cdots + d(N)^2)}{(N^3 - N)}$$

Does `Spearman` compute this value? It appears that `Spearman` performs the first step, if we accept that `dvalue[X][i]` is x_{i+1} and `dvalue[Y][i]` is y_{i+1}. (We have no idea yet how the data are stored in `dvalue`, and indeed what the meanings of X and Y are.) We can sleuth `rank_data` to verify that ranks are assigned correctly. It appears that `Spearman` performs the second and third steps. The last loop and the expression following it make this evident.

SLEUTHING RULE 3

We summarize the kind of reasoning activity illustrated above as: Understand the application. Become conversant in the jargon of the application to prepare yourself for intelligent dialogue with experts.

2.4 Conclusions

If the sleuth initiates the sleuthing process using the guidelines above, he or she will find that two of the major obstacles to understanding programs have been successfully confronted: language and application. These obstacles having been removed, the sleuth can tackle the more subtle structural issues of modularization and algorithm and data structures without the distractions of language and application-specific details.

▶▶▶▶▶ *Exercises*

2–1. Do you know your FORTRAN? State the effect of the following program fragment. How do you know your answer is correct?

```
        IF (I.GT.0) THEN
   1    TYPE *,'YES'
        ELSE
        IF (J.GT.0) GOTO 1
        TYPE *,'NO'
        ENDIF
```

2–2. Do you know your C? Repeat Exercise 2–1 for this program fragment:

```
int x[4] = {0, 0, 0, 0}, *px;
px = x;
```

```
px++;
*px++;
```

2–3. Do you know the differences between FORTRAN and C? Compare and contrast the following two program fragments.

C program fragment:

```
x = 1;
clear (x);
printf ("%d\n", x);
```

FORTRAN program fragment:

```
X = 1
CALL CLEAR (X)
TYPE *,X
```

2–4. "Knowing your application" can greatly improve your understanding of a program.

    a. Without consulting any suggested readings, determine what the following FORTRAN program fragment does:

```
IF (B.GT.0) THEN
    IF (B*B.GT.4*C) THEN
        TYPE *,'OVERDAMPED'
    ELSEIF (B*B.EQ.4*C) THEN
        TYPE *,'CRITICALLY DAMPED'
    ELSE
        TYPE *,'UNDERDAMPED'
    ENDIF
ELSEIF (B.EQ.0) THEN
    TYPE *,'MARGINALLY STABLE'
ELSE
    TYPE *,'UNSTABLE'
ENDIF
```

    b. Now consult a text on linear systems and revise (if necessary) your explanation of what the program fragment does. (We list some texts in the suggested readings.) In what ways did knowing the application change your explanation?

2–5. Repeat Exercise 2–4 for the following C program fragment. This time, you can learn about your application in a text on algorithms and data structures, some of which we list in the suggested readings.

```
n++;
i = n-1;
while (i > 0) {
```

```
if (x[i/2] > x[i]) {
    t = x[i/2]; x[i/2] = x[i]; x[i] = t;
}
i = i/2;
}
```

2-6. Repeat Exercise 2-4 for the following FORTRAN program fragment, this time with a text on digital simulation. (Again, see the suggested readings.)

```
U1 = RAN(Z)
U2 = RAN(Z)
X1 = SQRT(-2*LOG(U1)) * COS(2*PI*U2)
X2 = SQRT(-2*LOG(U1)) * SIN(2*PI*U2)
```

By the way, do you know your FORTRAN? What is the RAN subroutine? (It's not standard.)

2-7. Describe the effect of these two procedures in STATS.C:

a. Wilcoxon

b. Kruskal_Wallis

2-8. How does the procedure rank_data in the file STATS.C assign ranks to elements with the same value? Compare this with the definition of the Spearman, Wilcoxon, or Kruskal-Wallis test statistics.

▶ ▶ ▶ ▶ ▶ *Problems*

2-1. Go through the language reference manual for your favorite high-level language. Identify those statements and language facilities (e.g., run-time library) you use regularly, those you use on occasion, and those you never use. What percentage of language facilities belong to each category? Can you now say that you are an "expert" in the language?

2-2. Repeat Problem 2-1, but now identify those features that appear to be machine-independent and those that are not. To do this you will probably need language manuals for several different computer systems. How much of the programs that you write are portable from one computer system to another?

2-3. In how many different application areas have you successfully written programs? For each area, how did you solve the "know the application" problem?

2-4. A key issue in language choice is expressive power. Compare the ability of four or five languages of your choice (we recommend at least FORTRAN, C, assembler, and an object-oriented language) to handle the following types of operations or structures:

- linear array processing
- linked list manipulations
- stack operations
- dynamic storage allocation
- file management
- I/O operations
- recursive procedures
- operations on mixed data types
- algebraic and trigonometric computations

Do you think any one language is the best overall? Explain why or why not.

2–5. Discuss the possible relevance of directory names to understanding the organization of files that make up a program. We will revisit this problem after we have looked at the Statistics/Graphics Program further.

2–6. We posed four questions about the Statistics/Graphics Program in Section 2.3. Suggest four more.

Suggested Readings

Understanding language and application is a broad-based endeavor. Here we list a few references. The "K & R standard" C reference is Kernighan and Ritchie's book (1978). It has since been revised to the ANSI standard (1988).

For chemistry, we suggest Rosenberg's outline (1980) and the college-level textbooks by Hein (1986) and Kroschwitz and Winokur (1987). Each provides the background for the ORBIT program.

Spearman, Kruskal-Wallis and Wilcoxon statistics seem to be more common in older statistics texts such as those by Duckworth (1968) and Siegel (l956). Not all three statistics are found in every text. The Statistics/Graphics Program's user's manual references the text by Siegel, which does define all three.

One basic linear systems reference is Close and Frederick's text (1978).

Among the many good texts on algorithms and data structures are Knuth's classic series (1973a, 1973b, 1981), the "AHU" books (Aho, Hopcroft, and Ullman 1974, 1985), and a comprehensive new book by Cormen, Leiserson, and Rivest (1990). Sedgewick's popular texts (1988, 1990) are also nice references.

For digital simulation, we suggest any of the following: Neelamkavil's book (1987), Payne's book (1982), Pritsker's introduction to the simulation language SLAM II (1986), and Law and Kelton's text (1982).

References

Aho, Alfred V., John E. Hopcroft, and Jeffrey D. Ullman. *Data Structures and Algorithms.* Reading, MA: Addison-Wesley, 1985.

Aho, Alfred V., John E. Hopcroft, and Jeffrey D. Ullman. *The Design and Analysis of Computer Algorithms.* Reading, MA: Addison-Wesley, 1974.

Close, C. M., and D. K. Frederick. *Modeling and Analysis of Dynamic Systems.* Boston: Houghton-Mifflin, 1978.

Cormen, Thomas H., Charles E. Leiserson, and Ronald L. Rivest. *Introduction to Algorithms.* New York: McGraw-Hill, 1990.

Duckworth, W. E. *Statistical Techniques in Technological Research.* London: Methuen, 1968.

Hein, Morris. *Foundations of College Chemistry.* 6th ed. Monterey, CA: Brooks/Cole, 1986.

Kernighan, B. W., and D. Ritchie. *The C Programming Language.* Englewood Cliffs, NJ: Prentice-Hall, 1978.

Kernighan, B. W., and D. Ritchie. *The C Programming Language.* 2d ed. Englewood Cliffs, NJ: Prentice-Hall, 1988.

Knuth, Donald E. *Fundamental Algorithms.* Vol. 1 of *The Art of Computer Programming.* 2d ed. Reading, MA: Addison-Wesley, 1973.

Knuth, Donald E. *Seminumerical Algorithms.* Vol. 2 of *The Art of Computer Programming.* 2d ed. Reading, MA: Addison-Wesley, 1981.

Knuth, Donald E. *Sorting and Searching.* Vol. 3 of *The Art of Computer Programming.* Reading, MA: Addison-Wesley, 1973.

Kroschwitz, Jacqueline, and Melvin Winokur. *Chemistry: A First Course.* 2d ed. New York: McGraw-Hill, 1987.

Law, Averill M., and W. David Kelton. *Simulation Modeling and Analysis.* New York: McGraw-Hill, 1982.

Neelamkavil, Francis. *Computer Simulation and Modelling.* Chichester/Sussex, England: Wiley, 1987.

Payne, James A. *Introduction to Simulation.* New York: McGraw-Hill, 1982.

Pritsker, A. Alan B. *Introduction to Simulation and SLAM II.* 3d ed. New York: Wiley, 1986.

Rosenberg, Jerome L. *Schaum's Outline of College Chemistry.* 6th ed. New York: McGraw-Hill, 1980.

Sedgewick, Robert. *Algorithms.* 2d ed. Reading, MA: Addison-Wesley, 1988.

Sedgewick, Robert. *Algorithms in C.* Reading, MA: Addison-Wesley, 1990.

Siegel, S. *Nonparametric Statistics for the Behavioral Sciences.* New York: McGraw-Hill, 1956.

3
Modularization: Figuring Out
How the Software Was Pieced Together

Once the software sleuth begins to look at the actual program itself, the first step is to understand the organization and interrelationships of the various modules comprising the software. This chapter focuses on this all-important topic.

In Section 3.1 we describe the general process of looking for modularization. This is followed in Sections 3.2 and 3.3 by a more detailed discussion of two key issues in module sleuthing: determining which modules are important and appreciating how the program was modularized. We illustrate these principles in the context of both the Statistics/Graphics Program and simpler stand-alone examples. We take an intuitive, nontechnical approach; for formal approaches to software engineering issues such as modular coupling, module interdependence, and data abstraction, we refer you to the suggested readings.

3.1 Looking for Modular Structure

Let us assume that the original programmers had an internal sense of *modularity*. Thus they approached problem-solving by breaking things up into manageable pieces. In the context of programming this means that the program consists of a number of essentially independent

▶**Figure 3–1   A Calling Net**

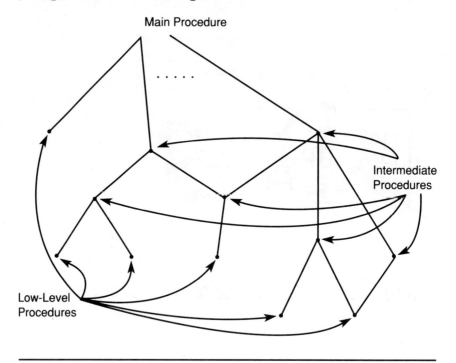

parts connected to each other by (conditional) branches or procedure calls. Defining what, if any, modular structure is present is a basic part of the software sleuthing process. At the most rudimentary level it involves the following actions:

▶ Identifying all the distinct subprograms, or procedures, that comprise the source program.

▶ For each procedure, making a list showing which procedures it calls and which data items are passed either as arguments or through shared storage (e.g., COMMON blocks, global variables).

▶ Using the above information to construct a calling net: a list showing the potential calls between all the procedures in the program. The calling net can be viewed graphically as well (see Figure 3–1).

When the above steps have been completed the sleuth has obtained some useful information about the program's organization, as well as some insight into local and shared data areas. One of the interesting perspectives the calling net can give the sleuth is an idea of what is at the top (the main procedure in a program) and what is at the bottom (usually many procedures). When it comes time to study algorithms and data structures, the sleuth will have two obvious ways to begin: *top down* and *bottom up*.

The sleuth can begin top down by scanning the main procedure. This usually gives the sleuth a sense of the key actions of the software, along with the sequence in which second-level and still lower-level procedures are called.

The sleuth can also begin bottom up, looking at procedures that call no others. Usually these procedures are of a utility nature; understanding their operation is generally straightforward. Understanding their purpose in the overall scheme of things is often difficult, though every effort must be made to do so. Understanding a procedure's purpose enhances understanding of the procedure itself.

By following the approach sketched above the sleuth can get a good intuitive understanding of many procedures that comprise the overall program. Only the intermediate nodes in the calling net graph have been unexplored. Of course, it is usually the middle-level procedures that tell the sleuth the most about what the program is doing. In Section 3.2 we give some general ideas on how to determine which of the middle-level procedures are most important.

Example 3–1

A Program with an Ideal Modular Structure

Consider the idealized situation in which each procedure, including the main program, calls N distinct procedures until the bottom level, which is the Lth in the tree. Assume $N > 1$. In other words, the calling net is a full N-ary tree with L levels (see Figure 3–2).

The total number of procedures (including the main program) in this simple model is

$$1 + N + N^2 + \ldots + N^{L-1} = (N^L - 1)/(N - 1)$$

Of these, $N^{L-1} + 1$ are at the top or bottom level. Thus, studying the top- and bottom-level procedures would give us an understanding of the following fraction of all procedures:

$$\frac{(N^{L-1} + 1)(N - 1)}{(N^L - 1)}$$

which is approximately $(N-1)/N$. If $N = 3$ and $L = 5$, for example, there are 121 total procedures, of which 82 are either top level or bottom level. Thus the sleuth could gain an understanding of more than two-thirds of the procedures present by constructing a calling net and studying the top- and bottom-level procedures!

There is a disclaimer, of course. Since the calling net usually is not a tree, the fraction of procedures that are top or bottom level may not be so high. But see Problem 3–1.

▶Figure 3–2   A Full *N*-ary Tree with *L* Levels

Number of Nodes

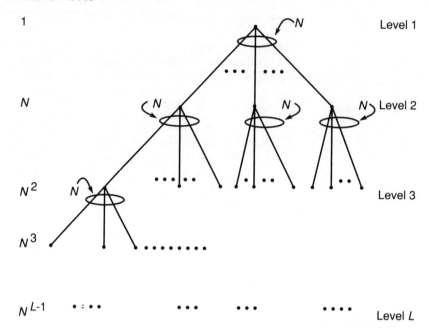

1   Level 1

N Level 2

N^2 Level 3

N^3

N^{L-1} Level L

Example 3–2

MINSORT's Modular Structure

MINSORT's calling net is shown in Figure 3–3. It has five procedures, four of which are either top or bottom level.

▶Figure 3–3   MINSORT's Calling Net

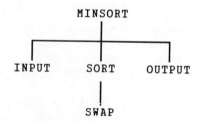

Example 3–3

The Statistics/Graphics Program's Modular Structure

Let us now try to understand, in a general way, the modular structure of the Statistics/Graphics Program. During our actual sleuthing of this program, a complete calling net (involving *every* procedure) was not needed right away because our initial sleuthing required only that we understand the most obvious errors in the program. In fact the very first "detection" required was to correct an error in the entry of floating point data items in the spreadsheet: Values were always being displayed as a fixed number regardless of the actual input. (Note that practical sleuthing often is initially motivated by finding causes of errors. This may allow us to sleuth limited sections of the program at first—although to feel truly comfortable with any changes we ultimately make, more detailed knowledge of the program is invariably needed.)

The calling sequence leading to the error is shown in Figure 3–4. We found the error to be the omission of the function prototype for the C library function `atof`; `wgetf` was treating the return value of `atof` as the data type `int`, not as the data type `float`, which for various reasons related to data representation resulted in the symptom we observed. At this point, we had the beginnings of a calling net and as we continued to sleuth, our calling net grew larger.

In the remainder of this example, we take a slightly different approach and show how the sleuth, looking for no error in particular, might collect the data needed to construct a meaningful calling net. Be aware that we are restricting our attention to the procedures in Appendix B—less than half the Statistics/Graphics Program.

Files and Procedures

The sleuth can begin constructing the calling net by preparing a list of the procedures in each file. This will be helpful later in finding modules. The organization of procedures into files may also give some clues about the program. The various software tools described in Appendix A are well suited to aid in preparing this list. We found in this instance that the load map generated by Microsoft's linker gave the information we needed.

▶ **Figure 3–4   Calling Sequence from main to atof**

Procedure	File
main	MAIN.C
flow_control	FLOW.C
menu_3	MENU_003.C
modify	MENU_003.C
wgetf	(not listed)
atof	(run-time library)

Tables 3–1 and 3–2 give two versions of this list of procedures. The first arranges the procedures alphabetically by file (and by order of appearance within the file), the second arranges them alphabetically by name. We have omitted some information about the files that actually is quite rich—the subdirectories in which the files were found. (There were four: the root, \MENUS, \GRAPHS, and \RECORDS.) Problem 3–2 explores this type of information further.

▶ **Table 3–1   Procedures in the Statistics/Graphics Program Sorted by File (Partial List)**

File	Module
AXIS.C	display_message
	display_title
	round
	load_labels
	load_ordinal_labels
	plot_y_axis
	ordinal_x_axis
	plot_x_axis3
DISPLAY.C	dump_screen
	print_graph
	view
	init_graphics
	restore_graphics
	show_graph
	get_user_y_range
	get_user_x_range
	g_write
	graph_message
	graph_inquire
	get_string
	get_chart_size
	.
	.
	.
VIEWPORT.C	setup_limits
	setup_y_limits
	setup_x_limits
	use_plotting_limits
	world_to_screen
	clipv
	set_window
	set_viewport
	set_window_viewport

▶ **Table 3–2   Procedures in the Statistics/Graphics Program Sorted by Name (Partial List)**

Module	File
add_link	RECORDS.C
add_record	MENU_003.C
advance_cursor	MENU_003.C
before_after	MENU_003.C
call_export_data	MENU_000.C
call_restore_session	MENU_000.C
call_save_session	MENU_000.C
change_date	MENU_006.C
change_groups	MENU_003.C
clear_all	MAIN.C
clear_data	MAIN.C
clear_data_sets	MAIN.C
clear_dine_arrays	IO.C
clear_flag	MAIN.C
clear_name	MENU_006.C
clear_parameter_fields	MENU_003.C
clear_parameters	MENU_002.C
clear_screen	MAIN.C
.	
.	
.	
warning	MAIN.C
world_to_screen	VIEWPORT.C
x_axis	INDIVID.C
y_axis	INDIVID.C

File Calling Net

Since the Statistics/Graphics Program is quite large (there are 18 files and 126 procedures in Appendix B and not everything is listed) the sleuth may find it

more reasonable at first to construct a *file calling net* by considering the whole file as one module. Thus "FILE1.C" calls "FILE2.C" if any procedure in "FILE1.C" calls a procedure in "FILE2.C." Such a graph is shown in Figure 3–5. You are given an opportunity in Exercise 3–5 to construct a procedure calling net for the Statistics/Graphics Program.

SLEUTHING RULE 4

Look for modular structure. List procedures or files in the program and construct a calling net or related structure to get a basic feeling for relationships among procedures or files.

▶Figure 3–5   **Statistics/Graphics Program File
Calling Net (Some Details Omitted)**

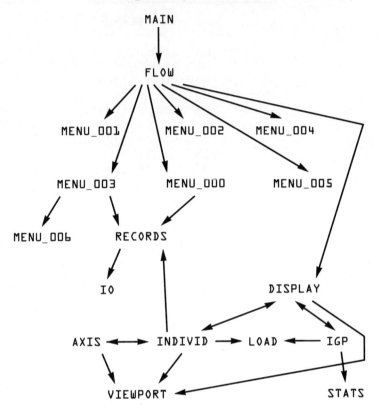

3.2 Determining Which Modules Are Important

In Section 3.1 we said that top-level and bottom-level modules in a calling net are important. Now we discuss the question, "What other ones are important?" In the absence of goals such as finding the source of an error (as we did in Example 3–3), we suggest the following guidelines.

1. Modules called by many others are important.

2. Modules that call many others are important.

3. Modules that "bridge" two parts of the calling net are important (there's a way to state this formally, but a visual indication is usually sufficient).

4. Modules whose names sound important might be important.

The last guideline seems simplistic, but it is worth considering. A good programmer's naming conventions should extend from variable names to procedure names to file names. Determining which modules are important is relevant only for larger programs for which not all modules can be studied in detail, so we focus only on the Statistics/Graphics Program.

There certainly may be some important modules that are called only once and call only one other. As you begin to understand a program the idea of "importance" will change, but our suggestions should result in a reasonable first cut.

Example 3–4

Important Modules in the Statistics/Graphics Program

The file calling net for the Statistics/Graphics Program (Figure 3–5) gives the following clues about the program's organization.

Clue 1   The most important file seems to be `FLOW.C` because it fans out from `MAIN.C` to many other files (and most of their names begin with `MENU`).

Clue 2   The files `MENU_xxx.C` seem quite important, related to various display menus, with `MENU_000.C` and `MENU_003.C` somewhat higher in level in the file calling net.

Clue 3   The file `DISPLAY.C` seems important, as it bridges together two portions of the file calling net.

Clue 4   Among low-level files referenced by many others, and thus apparently important, are `RECORDS.C` and `VIEWPORT.C`.

These clues provide some initial answers to the questions posed earlier in Section 2.3. Concerning choice of menus, `FLOW.C` should give some information, since it references most `MENU_xxx.C` files. Concerning graphs, we might study `DIS-PLAY.C`, and concerning statistics, we might study `STATS.C` (note how names play an important role in the sleuthing process). Concerning the spreadsheet, `MENU_000.C` and `MENU_003.C` might be worth examining, if only for the reason that they reference `RECORDS.C` (again the name). Finally, the sleuth might want to study `RECORDS.C` itself.

The above discussion is couched in terms of files and not their contained procedures per se. Once the important files have been identified, we can repeat the above process on the procedures.

SLEUTHING RULE 5

Determine which modules are important. Identify key modules in the calling net by looking for those that call many others or are called by many others, or that "bridge" together two parts of the calling net. Pay particular attention to names.

3.3 Appreciating the Choice of Modularization

The advantages of modular design are well known to software engineers. How to modularize—by stepwise refinement, data abstraction, a transform-centered approach, or a host of other ways—has long been a topic of study, research, and teaching in software engineering. The modern object-oriented programming environment extends data abstraction even further. The interested reader can find references to some of the alternatives in the suggested reading.

Since programs are likely to be modularized in any of the standard ways—or all of them—the software sleuth must intuitively understand the kinds of modular structure that are likely to be present in programs and the ways in which modules are coupled. An informal discussion of this issue is given below.

The method of modularization is often hard to determine; it may require an understanding of the specifications of the procedures, something the sleuth learns only gradually. The important point, though, is to try to appreciate the original programmer's approach. This will often give insight into unexplored parts of the program, even to the point of understanding procedures just by their names.

We will illustrate these concepts using both MINSORT and the Statistics/Graphics Program.

Example 3–5

MINSORT's Modularization

Let us revisit MINSORT, whose calling net we studied in Example 3–2. MINSORT's modularization is a small-scale example of the transform-centered approach: INPUT reads the data, SORT "transforms" it, and OUTPUT writes the result. If MINSORT were part of a larger program, the sleuth might expect to see other input-transform-output sequences. MINSORT's main program also illustrates clearly the idea of stepwise refinement.

Example 3–6

A Variant of MINSORT and Its Modularization

Consider the program MINSORT–II (Figure 3–6), which has a main program and three procedures. (Note that we have intentionally introduced a "variation" in the implementation compared to MINSORT. Sleuthing cannot depend on consistency of implementation and the sleuth must be prepared to see various flavors of the same algorithms, even within a single program structure.)

▶ Figure 3–6 MINSORT-II Program

```
      PROGRAM MINSORT
C
      INTEGER A(100),PLACE
C
      CALL INPUT(A,N)
C
      DO 1000 I = 1,N-1
C
      MIN = A(I)
      PLACE = I
C
      DO 500 J = I+1,N
C
      IF(A(J).LT.MIN) THEN
          PLACE = J
          MIN = A(J)
      ENDIF
C
500   CONTINUE
C
      CALL SWAP(A,N,I,PLACE)
C
1000  CONTINUE
C
      CALL OUTPUT(A,N)
      STOP
      END
C
C     INPUT module --------------------------------
C
      SUBROUTINE INPUT(A,N)
      INTEGER  A(N)
C
      TYPE *, 'PLEASE ENTER LIST TO BE SORTED'
      TYPE *, 'ENTER LENGTH OF LIST, THEN LIST'
      ACCEPT *, N
      ACCEPT *, (A(K),K = 1,N)
      TYPE *, ' '
      TYPE *, 'ORIGINAL LIST IS ' ! ECHO LIST BACK
      TYPE *, (A(K),K = 1,N)
      RETURN
      END
```

continued

▶ **Figure 3–6**—*Continued*

```
C
C      OUTPUT module -------------------------------
C
       SUBROUTINE OUTPUT(A,N)
       INTEGER A(N)
C
       TYPE *, 'SORTED LIST IS'
       TYPE *, (A(K),K = 1,N)
       RETURN
       END
C
C      SWAP module ---------------------------------
C
       SUBROUTINE SWAP(A,N,1,PLACE)
       INTEGER A(N),PLACE,TEMP
C
       TEMP = A(I)
       A(I) = A(PLACE)
       A(PLACE) = TEMP
C
       RETURN
       END
```

How would the sleuth reason on seeing `MINSORT-II`? The partitioning involves separate procedures for input and output. There is also a procedure for swapping two list elements. The experienced software sleuth might proceed as follows:

"I'll first draw up a calling net of the program (Figure 3–7). This is easy to do since the net is a tree with two levels. I'll then note what arguments are passed between each call—this identifies the data flow. The issue of global and local variables is irrelevant here, since all variables are passed as arguments—nothing is shared in common storage."

Here the modularization is more of a utility nature. `MINSORT-II`'s main program controls the flow with the help of `INPUT`, `OUTPUT`, and `SWAP`. If `MINSORT-II` were part of a larger program the sleuth might expect to see some relatively complex high-level procedures and relatively simple low-level ones.

▶ **Figure 3–7   MINSORT-II's Calling Net**

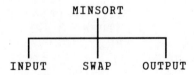

Example 3–7

The Statistics/Graphics Program's Modularization

We finally consider the Statistics/Graphics Program to try to see what kind of modularization it has—and we will need to get ahead of ourselves somewhat to do so. In Chapter 4 we will see that among the data types in the program only one is "abstract," namely RECORD, so data abstraction is not the only method. The modularization could be considered transform-centered in the following sense: For each menu or data entry screen in the Statistics/Graphics Program there is a set of procedures that apply transformations to the data. There are also elements of stepwise refinement, both at high levels (e.g., flow_control, Example 4–2) and low levels (e.g., calls to t_getkey, Example 4–1).

As a general rule it does not appear that the original programmers followed a system of modularization. The clues that the Statistics/Graphics Program gives about the original programmers show that they were mostly interested in the individual menus or screens and not so much in how data are represented. The sleuth would need to think step by step, screen by screen, the same way a beginning user would approach the program.

SLEUTHING RULE 6

Appreciate the method of modularization. Be sensitive to the types of modules present and the coupling between them. Try to understand how the original programmers preferred to solve their programming problems.

3.4 Conclusions

The second phase of sleuthing involves issues related to modular organization. The sleuth must understand how the program is pieced together from various modules and how data and control are passed back and forth between modules. Once this is done the sleuth can begin to unravel the individual modules. The top and bottom levels of the calling net provide a wealth of modules to consider first.

▶ ▶ ▶ ▶ ▶ Exercises

3–1. We have shown the calling net for the MINSORT–II program. Draw a "data flow" net for it that shows which variables are passed between procedures and which of those variables are modified. What are the data types of the variables?

3–2. Repeat Exercise 3–1 for MINSORT.

3–3. We gave an incomplete listing of procedures sorted by file for the Statistics/Graphics Program in Table 3–1. Complete it, using the listings of Appendix B. (Actually, since these listings are not *all* the listings of the Statistics/Graphics Program, your list is still incomplete, but certainly more extensive than the one given in the text.) Are any of the tools of Appendix A useful here?

3–4. Repeat Exercise 3–3 for the alphabetical version of the procedure listings, using Table 3–2 as a starting point. Are any of the tools of Appendix A useful here?

3–5. Refer to Exercises 3–3 and 3–4. Now that you have a list of all the procedures in Appendix B, take the first step in producing a calling net for the Statistics/Graphics Program by listing, for each procedure, which procedures it potentially calls. Some potentially called procedures may not be listed in Appendix B. What is the approximate depth of the partial net you have constructed?

► ► ► ► ► *Problems*

3–1. Choose several programs written by yourself or by someone else. Construct the calling net for each such program. Is it a tree structure, or some more complex graph? What percentage of the procedures comprise the top and bottom levels of the net? How does this compare to the 82/121 figure given in Example 3–1?

3–2. Discuss the relevance of directory names and directory structure in understanding the logical organization of the files that make up the Statistics/Graphics Program.

3–3. Investigate some commonly used graphical devices for specifying calling structures and discuss which ones might give the clearest information about the Statistics/Graphics Program.

3–4. What do you think the terms *module fan-out* and *module fan-in* mean? Why is this important to the software sleuth?

3–5. Comment on the discussion in Example 3–7 of the modularization of the Statistics/Graphics Program. What other kinds of modularization do you see in the program?

3–6. Discuss the differences between sleuthing a "monolithic" program consisting of only one module and a program with the same function modularized according to one of the modern software engineering techniques. What are the challenges the sleuth faces in each case? How does this motivate you to solve your future programming problems?

Suggested Readings

Modularization has been one of the central issues of programming methodology because it concerns not only programming but also managing programmers. One good high-level survey is by Yau and Tsai (1986).

Among the earliest and best references on this topic are books by Yourdon and Constantine (1979) and Myers (1978). These develop the composite or transform-centered approach in which a problem is divided into input, transformation, and output subproblems, which themselves are further subdivided the same way. Such terms as *module coupling* and *module interdependence* are also found in Myers's book.

Wirth had earlier discussed the methodology called stepwise refinement (1971). In this method a program is designed from the top down, each level revealing greater detail. Parnas (1972) showed how the principle of information hiding—leaving data representations as details local to a few modules—could make a program easier to maintain.

Data abstraction is a relatively new approach to modularization (compared to the other approaches). A good research reference on the theory behind data abstraction can be found in Danforth and Tomlinson's review article (1988). Liskov and Guttag based an entire language (CLU) on this method (1986). Another nice survey is the one by Shaw (1984), which gives a practical overview of abstraction in modern programming languages. Object-oriented programming is the focus of Cox's text (1986).

Two other references of interest are an empirical study showing the effects of modularization on program maintenance (Korson and Vaishnavi 1986) and a program (with a formal proof that it is correct) that constructs calling nets for programs written in a dialect of FORTRAN (Ryder 1979).

References

Cox, B. J. *Object-Oriented Programming: An Evolutionary Approach.* Reading, MA: Addison-Wesley, 1986.

Danforth, Scott, and Chris Tomlinson. Type theories and object-oriented programming. *ACM Computing Surveys* 20:29–72, March 1988.

Korson, Timothy D., and Vijay K. Vaishnavi. An empirical study of the effects of modularity on program modifiability. In E. Soloway and S. Iyengar, editors, *Empirical Studies of Programmers*, pp. 168–186. Norwood, NJ: Ablex Publishing Corp., 1986.

Liskov, Barbara, and John Guttag. *Abstraction and Specification in Program Development.* Cambridge, MA: MIT Press, 1986.

Myers, G. J. *Composite/Structured Design.* New York: Van Nostrand-Reinhold, 1978.

Parnas, D. L. On the criteria to be used in decomposing systems into modules. *Communications of the ACM* 15:1053–1058, December 1972.

Ryder, B. G. Constructing the call graph of a program. *IEEE Transactions on Software Engineering* SE-5:216–225, May 1979.

Shaw, M. Abstraction techniques in modern programming languages. *IEEE Software* 1(4):10–26, October 1984.

Wirth, Niklaus. Program development by stepwise refinement. *Communications of the ACM* 14:221–227, April 1971.

Yau, Stephen S., and Jeffery J. Tsai. A survey of software design techniques. *IEEE Transactions on Software Engineering* SE-12:713–721, June 1986.

Yourdon, Edward, and Larry L. Constantine. *Structured Design.* Englewood Cliffs, NJ: Prentice-Hall, 1979.

Algorithms and Data Structures: Looking Inside the Modules

Once the sleuth has identified the modular structure underlying the program, he or she can begin to study the algorithms and data structures used in implementing the various modules. We turn to this next. As in the previous chapters, we will illustrate our techniques with the Statistics/ Graphics Program and with simpler examples.

Our discussion is divided into four parts. We begin with an overview of techniques for identifying key control structures. We discuss how to unravel algorithms, then data structures. Finally we note the importance of sleuthing the variables in a program.

The sleuth who is well versed in the modern theories of software engineering is at a great advantage in looking at the modules. Such a sleuth knows how to unravel poorly engineered programs better than sleuths not so well versed, just as a native English language speaker can unravel English slang and poor usage much more easily than a nonnative speaker.

4.1 Identifying Key Control Structures

A program is seldom executed in linear order. It is usually replete with branches, both conditional and unconditional, which cause the flow of

45

control to be changed. The sleuth can study the control flow of a procedure by means of a schematic program graph such as the one for the SORT procedure of MINSORT shown in Figure 4–1.

Program graph analysis is most useful at the procedure level, since the graphs tend to be very large—and thus lose their visual advantages—

▶ **Figure 4–1   Program Graph for SORT**

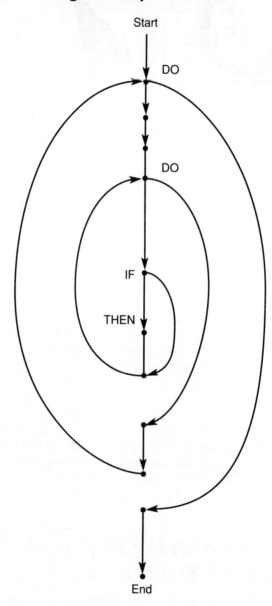

when drawn for a complete program. Constructing such graphs is often a challenge in itself; the sleuth must recognize the presence of control structures that are implicitly, not explicitly, embedded in the program. This is particularly true in unstructured languages.

There are many graphical and tabular means for specifying control structures. Our discussion below, for simplicity's sake, is primarily couched in terms of program graphs. Flow tables and state diagrams, two alternate schemes, are shown in Figure 4–2 and Table 4–1 below. For further discussion, we refer you to the suggested readings.

Clearly one of the sleuth's first steps in studying a program is to determine the structure of its program graphs, for their complexity tells a great deal about the complexity of the program itself. Formal graph-theoretic software metrics such as "cyclomatic complexity" can be applied here.

If the structure is linear—a graph without any branches at all—then there may actually be some merit in "reading the code from top to bottom," since the program is but a sequence of actions, all of which are unconditional. It is far more likely that, as in the case of MINSORT, there are various branches and loops. When such branches exist, the sharp software sleuth immediately gains some insight into the hitherto unknown functioning of the program. For example, if the sleuth observes that the value of a variable COUNT determines a branch, he or she can add COUNT to a growing list of clues about the program's behavior.

Generally one finds in program graphs two general types of structures besides the linear one (often termed the SEQUENCE structure). One is the IF-THEN-ELSE structure, the simple decision structure, often missing the ELSE portion. Multiway CASE structures are variants of this. The other is the structure that allows the conditional execution of a program loop, often called the DO-WHILE, DO-UNTIL, or simply ITERATIVE-DO structure. These are analyzed extensively in software engineering texts and the keen sleuth must be cognizant of their form and their presence.

We now give two examples from the Statistics/Graphics Program.

Example 4–1

MENU_003.C's Control Structures

Let us look at the control structures of a procedure in the file MENU_003.C. By constructing a calling net for the file MENU_003.C and discovering that the procedure menu_3 calls the largest number of procedures, the sleuth would have a clue that menu_3 is the most important.

menu_3's central control structure is a 19-way switch statement whose cases appear to correspond to keystrokes. A tabular approach is useful here, in view of the number of branches involved. Table 4–1 summarizes the cases.

The actions described in Table 4–1 make apparent the paths from menu_3 to other procedures. The paths are related to keyboard input

▶ **Table 4–1   Flow Table for menu_3**

Case	Apparent Key	Action
C_LEFT	left arrow	call `update_fields(-1)`
C_RIGHT	right arrow	call `update_fields(1)`
C_UP	up arrow	call `update_records(-1)`
C_DOWN	down arrow	call `update_records(1)`
HOME	home	set `record = u_record`
END	end	set `record = l_record`
F_1	function FI	call `help(4,0)`
F_2	function F2	call `before_after()` if `gdefs.analysis > 2`
F_3	function F3	call `change_groups()` if `gdefs.analysis = 4`
F_4	function F4	call `delete_record(current_scr)`
F_5	function F5	call `files_menu()` and possibly perform other steps
F_6	function F6	call `sort_records()` and set `REFRESH = 1`
F_7	function F7	call `dine_menu(current_scr, record)`
F_8	function F8	call `options_menu(current_scr, record)` and possibly perform other steps
F_9	function F9	call `change_directory()` and set `REFRESH = 1`
CR	enter	call `modify(current_scr)` and possibly call `advance_cursor()`; set `REFRESH = 1`
ESC	escape	set `ret_val = ESC`, exit loop
F_10	function FI0	set `ret_val = 0`
default	other	possibly call `modify(current_scr)`, among other steps

(apparently—we still do not know the function of `t_getkey`). Thus exercising the other procedures requires a state-based approach; first the state "menu_3" is entered and then one of 19 cases is selected with a keystroke. This is consistent with the observation made in Example 2–5 that the Statistics/Graphics Program is function-key driven.

The flow table immediately suggests a number of questions. What are the effects of `update_fields` and `update_records`? What are the meanings of the variables `record`, `u_record`, and `l_record`? What is the meaning of `gdefs.analysis`? We answer some of these questions in subsequent examples, leaving several others as exercises. See also Example 6–2.

Example 4–2

FLOW.C's Control Structures

Consider next the file `FLOW.C`. Its most important procedure is `flow_control`. `flow_control`'s central control structure is a 10-way CASE statement within a DO-WHILE loop. According to documentation within the file, `flow_control` "controls the overall flow from menu to menu using a finite automaton." It is not too hard to derive the state diagram of the finite automaton from the switch statement, although there are more states than the 10 cases. Figure 4–2 shows one such derivation. The state diagram shows what determines the sequence of menus in the Statistics/Graphics Program; thus it addresses, in part, one of our questions from Example 2–5, "What are the various menus and function keys and how are they related?"

SLEUTHING RULE 7

We have seen several alternate means of specifying control structures for sleuthing purposes: program graphs, flow tables, and state diagrams. Putting all of this together, we have this rule: Identify the key control structures in each module. Program graphs, flow tables, and state diagrams are among the schemes that highlight these constructs.

4.2 Unraveling the Algorithms

Having identified key control structures, the software sleuth is next faced with understanding the algorithms of the program at hand. Overly complex algorithms pose special difficulties of their own, but even straightforward algorithms may be hard to unravel if their implementation is haphazard or unstructured.

Often the sleuth must become a kind of copy editor, rewriting programs—at least on paper—to identify their underlying structure. As sleuths, we have often replaced large sections of so-called "spaghetti code" by structured pseudocode equivalents. The replacement often takes the form of supplementary in-line comments in the spaghetti code, since we are usually reluctant to change programs that more or less work.

▶ **Figure 4–2 State Diagram for flow_control**

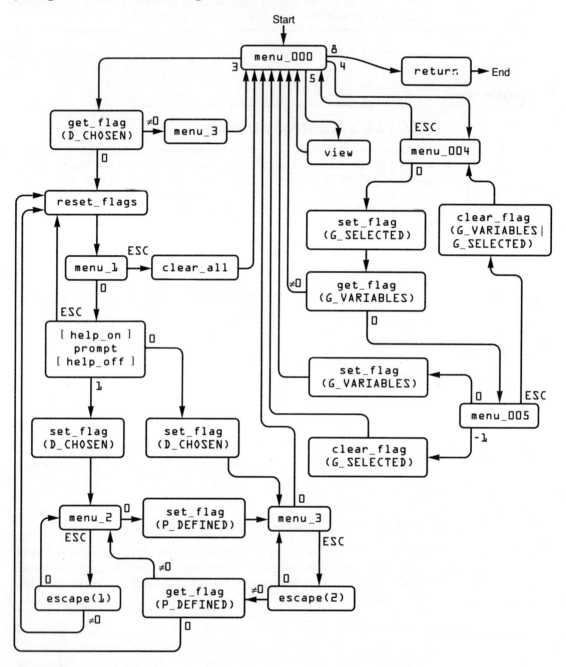

The interested reader will note that spaghetti code structure extends to the algorithms used to complete many of the common Internal Revenue Service tax forms. Perhaps, in some small way, this accounts for the complexity of completing income tax returns.

Unstructured programs are not the only ones the sleuth must unravel. Esoteric approaches, the product of creative and skilled programmers, present problems as well.

Among the esoteric approaches the sleuth might encounter are self-modifying code that literally rewrites parts of itself while executing; exotic, rare, powerful instructions and constructs seldom used by the average programmer because of their complexity; elaborate data structures; and subroutines that are jumped to, not called. Programmers' justifications for these approaches are myriad. A few examples:

▶ "It saves a few bytes of memory."

▶ "It saves a few microseconds of execution time."

▶ "It makes the program more secure from casual modification."

By and large, however, these cases are exceptional, but the astute software sleuth must deal with them and make mundane the overly subtle uses of language and algorithms. Sleuthing deals with all kinds of programs, not just those written in textbook fashion.

The sleuth should also be cognizant of error handling strategies while sleuthing programs. It is helpful to distinguish "normal" cases from "exceptional" ones and determine how the exceptional cases are handled.

Example 4–3

Two Quadratic Equation Programs and Their Algorithms

To gain more insight into unraveling algorithms, we look at a simple example of spaghetti code called QUADRA that finds the roots of a quadratic equation (Figure 4–3).

We can see by brief study that QUADRA appears to be computing the roots of the quadratic equation $Ax^2 + Bx + C = 0$ following the quadratic formula. It calls a function ROOT, which we assume returns the positive square root of a positive integer to some desired number of decimal places.

To understand why we call QUADRA spaghetti code, merely look at its program graph (Figure 4–4). If you squint, the graph looks like a plate full of spaghetti because of the numerous crossing arcs. (We have seen actual production-level software—software sold to clients—that looked no better than this. In fact, it looked far worse. Unfortunately it seemed to work. We say "seemed to" because it is hard to have confidence in such poorly constructed programs. Why "unfortunately"? If it did not work, then the programmers who wrote it might have had to reconsider their programming techniques, and could have avoided writing such monstrosities in the future.)

► Figure 4–3   **QUADRA Program**

```
            PROGRAM QUADRA
            INTEGER A,B,C,D
            TYPE *,'ENTER THE COEFFICIENTS'
            ACCEPT *, A,B,C
            IF(A.LE.0) GOTO 1200
            D = B**2 - 4*A*C
            IF(D.EQ.0) GOTO 52
            IF(D.LT.0) GOTO 800
C
C       D > 0 CASE -- TWO DISTINCT REAL ROOTS
C
            ROOT1 = (-B+ROOT(D))/(2*A)
            ROOT2 = (-B-ROOT(D))/(2*A)
            IF(ROOT1.LT.ROOT2) GOTO 56
            IF(ROOT1.GT.ROOT2) GOTO 33
56          TYPE *, 'THE ROOTS ARE BOTH REAL'
            TYPE *, 'THEY ARE ',ROOT1,ROOT2
            GOTO 805
33          TEMP = ROOT1
            ROOT1 = ROOT2
            ROOT2 = TEMP
            GOTO 56
C
C       D = 0 CASE -- TWO IDENTICAL REAL ROOTS
C
52          ROOT1 = -B/(2*A)
            TYPE *, 'THERE ARE TWO IDENTICAL REAL ROOTS'
            TYPE *, 'THE VALUE IS   ', ROOT1
            GOTO 805
C
C       D < 0 CASE -- ROOTS ARE COMPLEX CONJUGATES
C
800         ROOT1R = -B/(2*A)
            ROOT1I = ROOT(-D)/(2*A)
            ROOT2R = ROOT1R
            ROOT2I = -ROOT1I
            TYPE *, 'THE ROOTS ARE COMPLEX CONJUGATES'
            TYPE *, 'THEY ARE ',ROOT1R,' + I * ',ROOT1I
            TYPE *, 'AND ',ROOT2R,' + I * ',ROOT2I
            GOTO 805
C
1200    A <= 0 CASE -- RETURN WITH AN ERROR MESSAGE
C
            TYPE *,'A <= 0 -- NOT ALLOWED'
            STOP
C
805     STOP
            END
```

▶**Figure 4–4   QUADRA's Program Graph**

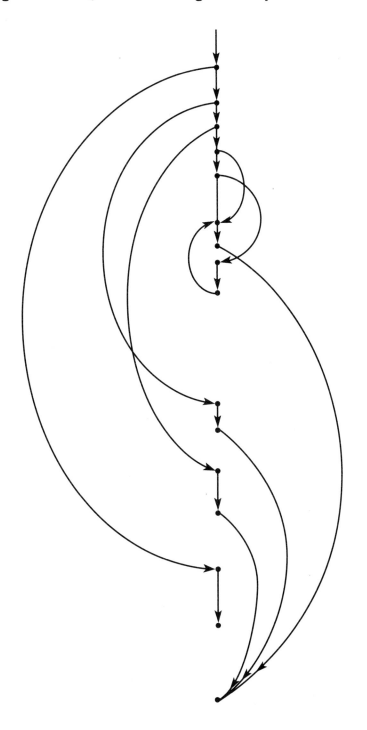

The basic problem with such convoluted code is that it is impossible to read, even by the programmer who wrote it. There is no orderly flow to the program and any bugs are very difficult to find.

A sleuth faced with a program like QUADRA may find it helpful to restructure the program so that it becomes readable and testable. Software engineering theory provides the ammunition with which to do this. A restructured version, QUADRA-II, is shown in Figure 4–5. This one is written using just two control structures—SEQUENCE and IF-THEN-ELSE. Its program graph is shown in Figure 4–6. Note the clarity of program control flow and the readability of the program.

There are a number of specific problems with QUADRA besides its terrible structure. It is inefficiently coded, for one thing. For example, there is no reason to have separate variables ROOT1R and ROOT2R. Inefficiencies have been greatly reduced in QUADRA-II; do any remain?

Problems 4–3 and 4–4 further dissect this example.

▶ Figure 4–5   QUADRA-II Program

```
PROGRAM QUADRA
INTEGER A,B,C,D
TYPE *,'ENTER THE COEFFICIENTS'
ACCEPT *, A,B,C
IF(A.LE.0) THEN
    TYPE *,'A <= 0 --NOT ALLOWED'
    STOP
ENDIF
D = B**2 - 4*A*C
IF(D.GT.0) THEN                  ! DISTINCT REAL ROOTS
    ROOT1 = (-B+ROOT(D))/(2*A)
    ROOT2 = (-B-ROOT(D))/(2*A)
    TYPE *,'THE ROOTS ARE BOTH REAL'
    TYPE *,'IN NUMERICAL ORDER THEY ARE'
    TYPE *,ROOT2,ROOT1
ELSE IF(D.EQ.0) THEN             ! IDENTICAL REAL ROOTS
        ROOT = -B/(2*A)
        TYPE *,'IDENTICAL REAL ROOTS'
        TYPE *,'VALUE IS  ',ROOT
    ELSE                        ! COMPLEX CONJ. ROOTS
        ROOTR = -B/(2*A)
        ROOTI = ROOT(D)/(2*A)
        TYPE *,'COMPLEX CONJUGATE ROOTS'
        TYPE *,'REAL PART IS  ',ROOTR
        TYPE *,'IMAGINARY PART IS  ',ROOTI
    ENDIF
ENDIF
STOP
END
```

▶Figure 4–6   QUADRA-II's Program Graph

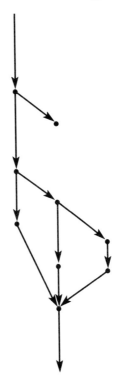

Example 4–4

modify's Algorithms

Let us now return to the Statistics/Graphics Program and address the question, "How are data files selected in the spreadsheet and what other items are entered?" Consider the procedure `modify` in `MENU_003.C`. The basic control structure is a nested IF-THEN-ELSE statement. This is already fairly structured. We give a flow table summarizing the control structure in Table 4–2.

As the flow table shows, `modify`'s action may include calling any of the following procedures: `select_data_file`, `perform_file_loading`, `wgetl` (perhaps "get long"?), `wgetf` (perhaps "get float"?), `category_menu`, and `message`.

The flow table provides further detail regarding the error we discussed in Example 3–3. We can see in `menu_3` that to enter `modify` involves selecting the `CR` or `default` case with a keystroke. From `modify`, to exercise `wgetf` requires the three conditions $window \neq 0$, $rec\_ptr{\to}day\_to\_use \neq 0$, and $params[p].ptype = 1$. But how are these conditions satisfied? More questions for the sleuth.

▶**Table 4–2 Flow Table for modify**

Condition	Action
window = 0, field = 0	call `select_data_file`, possibly call `perform_file_loading`
window = 0, field = I	call `wgetl` and possibly call `quick_load`, among other steps
window ≠ 0, rec_ptr->day_to_use ≠ 0, params[p].ptype = I	call `wgetf`, possibly change `rec_ptr->actual[FPM+p]`
window ≠ 0 rec_ptr->day_to_use ≠ 0, params[p].ptype ≠ I	possibly call `category_menu`, possibly change `rec_ptr->actual[FPM+p]`
window ≠ 0, rec_ ptr->day_to_use = 0	call `message` with an error message

Example 4–5

update_records' Algorithms

Continuing our discussion of the Statistics/Graphics Program's spreadsheet, we ask the question, "What is the effect of the procedure `update_records`?" To answer the question, we will need to unravel some nested IF-THEN statements. Although the procedure is structured (there are no GOTO statements), questions remain. The structure is not necessarily good.

Preliminary testing suggests that `update_records`' five outer IF-THEN statements respectively limit the number of records, handle the special case of advancing beyond the last record, keep the record index in range, scroll the spreadsheet up, and scroll the spreadsheet down. The first three are relatively straightforward, so we focus on the fourth and fifth.

The fifth IF-THEN statement,

```
if (get_row(record) < FR)
  {
    u_record--;
    if (u_record >= 0)
      {
        if (get_row(l_record) > LR) l_record--;
        scroll_fields_down(FR, LR, 1);
        redraw_record ( u_record);
      }
    else
      u_record++;
  }
```

is fairly complex, but "translation" simplifies it significantly. Consider the condition `get_row(record) < FR`. Expanding the definition of `get_row` we find that the condition is equivalent to `record < u_record`. Now `record` ≥ 0 or the third outer IF-THEN statement would have exited and the fifth IF-THEN statement would not have been reached. Thus the condition `u_record` ≥ 0 is implied by `get_row(record) < FR` (even if `u_record` is decremented first). The fifth IF-THEN statement can thus be rewritten with no change in effect by removing its inner IF-THEN statement to give the following:

```
if (get_row(record) < FR)
  {
    u_record--;
    if (get_row(l_record) > LR) l_record--;
    scroll_fields_down(FR,LR,1);
    redraw_record ( u_record);
  }
```

The rewritten statement makes the function clear: The statement scrolls the spreadsheet down and displays the newly selected record if the newly selected record is not visible. It also keeps `l_record` in range.

The fourth IF-THEN statement can also be simplified if we assume that `get_row(l_record)` $\leq$ `LR` whenever `update_records` is called. This is reasonable but requires some further analysis, which is left as Exercise 4–2.

Our "translation" has thus clarified the effect of `update_records`. But how do `scroll_fields_up`, `scroll_fields_down`, and `redraw_record` work? See Exercise 4–3.

SLEUTHING RULE 8

Summarizing all of this, we have our next rule: Unravel the algorithms, if only on paper. Try to reconstruct, with restructuring and inferential reasoning,, what the original programmer intended.

4.3 Unraveling the Data Structures

We now turn to data structures. The software sleuth is often involved in unraveling strangely defined data structures, particularly those implemented in high-level languages that do not directly support such structures well. FORTRAN is notorious in this respect, since pointers per se do not exist and array subscripts are often used as implicit pointers. Thus various artifices are used by programmers to create linked lists, for example.

Even in languages such as C that do support data structures well, the sleuth must ask what information is carried in each field of a structure. To the extent that data abstraction is present, primitive procedures operating on the data structures can also give clues. This is especially important in object-oriented languages for which the data types are the central part of the program. In general, one must be careful to distinguish between the abstract meaning of a data type (what it means to the program at large) and its concrete representation (how it is seen by the primitive procedures).

Here we will look at one example, the data structure or data type RECORD. We also examine the primitive procedures that operate on variables of that type.

Example 4–6

The RECORD Data Structure

We now address the question, "How are the data stored internally?" and turn to the file RECORDS.C for an answer.

Up to this point we have been looking primarily at control structures, but in the file RECORDS.C we are primarily looking at its data structure RECORD. For this it is helpful to look at the header file STRUCT.H in which the type RECORD is defined. Variables of type RECORD are found throughout the file RECORDS.C.

The type RECORD is defined as struct verify_ where verify_ is a 12-field C structure, summarized in Table 4–3.

We discuss four fields, focusing on the concrete representation of the data. The abstract meaning is quite similar, since the Statistics/Graphics Program has only a limited amount of data abstraction. Indeed, the only parts of the concrete representation not widely used outside RECORDS.C are the links that connect a list of records. The four fields are:

▶ next, previous—These are probably the links in a double-linked list, as study of the procedures new_record, add_link, and insert_link reveals.

▶ filename—new_record clears it, refresh_rec in MENU_003.C displays it, and modify in MENU_003.C passes it to quick_load. We assume

▶ Table 4–3   Fields of RECORD Structure

Field	Description (comments)
filename	(FileSize + 1) − character string
individual	31-character string (individual's name)
version	integer
day_to_use	integer
days_in_file	integer
weight	integer
actual	40-element real array (actual data values)
low	40-element floating-point array (recommended low range)
high	40-element floating-point array (recommended high range)
data	nine-character string
next	pointer to verify_ structure
previous	pointer to verify_ structure

`quick_load` loads nutritional data from the file whose file name is in this field.

▶ `weight`—This field is never used in any of the procedures listed in Appendix B; weight is instead stored in an element of the `actual` field (see Exercise 4–5).

Let's look at three of the primitive procedures in `RECORDS.C`:

▶ `new_record`—Apparently allocates memory for a new record and initializes its fields, returning a pointer to the record.

▶ `release_screen(s)`—For each group from 0 to `MaxGroups` − 1 frees the records in the linked list whose head is `vscreens[group][s]`. (But what is a group, and what does `s` mean?) `EXTERN.H` gives the dimensions of `vscreens`: `MaxGroups` and 2.

▶ `get_record(s,record)`—This procedure returns a pointer to a record in the linked list whose head is `vscreens[gdefs.group][s]`; the record is the one indexed by `get_record`'s second argument. This leads to another question: What is `gdefs.group`?

SLEUTHING RULE 9

Unravel the data structures. As with the algorithms, try to reconstruct, with inferential reasoning, what the original programmer intended.

4.4 Investigating the Variables

Program variables often provide a rich supply of information. In a "detective" sense the variables are couriers of information that is covert at first. Understanding what a variable means can be as helpful as understanding key control and data structures. And, unlike control and data structures, variables require no unraveling, just a lot of cross-referencing.

In this section we examine variables referenced in two files of the Statistics/Graphics Program: `MENU_003.C` and `FLOW.C`. The variables we study are global variables and two global "flags." We also look at a special type of variable—the value that a procedure returns.

Example 4–7

MENU_003.C's Variables

Three of the global variables in the file `MENU_003.C` are `record`, `u_record`, and `l_record`. What are their meanings?

A string search of `MENU_003.C` using a standard text editor reveals that `record` is a variable of type `int` and that it is referenced in the following procedures:

- ► `refresh`, where it is cleared.

- ► `menu_3`, where it is set to `u_record` and `l_record`, respectively, in cases `HOME` and `END`, and passed to `dine_menu` and `options_menu`, respectively, in cases `F_7` and `F_8`. It is also passed to `inverse_bar`.

- ► `update_records`, where `direction` is added to it and other operations are performed.

- ► `delete_record`, where it is passed to `get_record` and `get_row` (a macro), and possibly decremented or cleared.

- ► `modify`, where it is passed to `get_record`, `get_row`, and `redraw_record`.

- ► `perform_file_loading`, where it is passed to `get_record` and `redraw_record`.

(Be aware that the variable `record` on which `restore_screen` and a few other procedures operate is a dummy parameter, not the variable in which we are interested.)

The main clues about the meaning of `record` come from `update_records` and the calls to `get_record`. `update_records` adds -1 to `record` after the up arrow key is pressed and $+1$ after the down arrow key. The calls to `get_record` pass `record`. Based on this we may conclude that `record` is an integer index to a list of records.

What about `u_record` and `l_record`? Analysis of the `HOME` and `END` cases of `menu_3` suggests that `u_record` is the index of the first record visible on the screen and `l_record` the index of the last. (If they were indexes of the first and last records in the spreadsheet, would not the programmer have used something like `0` and `tot_records-1`?) This hypothesis is strengthened by the fact that `get_row(rec)` is a macro defined as `FR+rec-u_record`, and `FR`, according to comments in `MENU_003.C`, is the first row on the screen.

Example 4–8

Some Flags in FLOW.C

We last turn to `FLOW.C`. The state diagram of Figure 4–2 lets us determine the sequence of conditions that exercise a given procedure. To reach `menu_005`, for example, involves a return value of 4 from `menu_000`, a return value of 0 from `menu_004`, and a return value of 0 from `get_flag(G_VARIABLES)`. Sleuthing `get_flag` reveals that the "flags" such as `G_VARIABLES` are essentially global variables. So a good question for the sleuth is, "What are the meanings of the flags?" We focus on two flags, `G_SELECTED` and `P_DEFINED`.

All the information we now present can be found by searching the listings for references to `G_SELECTED` and `P_DEFINED`.

G_SELECTED

`flow_control` sets `G_SELECTED` when `menu_004` returns 0, which means that the user selected a graph type. `flow_control` clears the flag when `menu_005` returns -1 or `ESC`, which means that the user pressed the escape key or selected no variables. In `menu_000` the flag is tested when the user chooses the "view graph" command; if the flag is set, `menu_000` returns 5, otherwise `menu_000` displays a warning. `clear_data_sets` clears the flag explicitly and `reset_flags` clears the flag implicitly.

The conclusion: `G_SELECTED` is set if and only if the user has provided sufficient information for a graph to be viewed when the "menu_000" state is entered.

P_DEFINED

`flow_control` sets `P_DEFINED` when `menu_2` returns 0, which means that the user has defined additional parameters. `flow_control` tests the flag when `menu_3` returns ESC and `escape(2)` returns a nonzero value, which means that the user wants to exit the "menu_3" state prematurely. If the flag is set, `flow_control` enters the "menu_2" state, and if it is clear, the "menu_1" state. `escape(1)` also tests the flag.

Conclusion: `P_DEFINED` is set to indicate that a premature exit out of the "menu_3" state should lead to an entry into the "menu_2" state because parameters are defined. Now you know why sleuths get paid well.

Example 4–9

menu_xxx's Return Values

Let us look at return values of the `menu_xxx` procedures. We discuss `menu_000`, `menu_3`, and `menu_005` here, leaving several others for Exercise 4–8. (Yes, there is an inconsistency in the names of these procedures, e.g., `menu_3`, not `menu_003`. This kind of thing comes with the territory in sleuthing.) What we state comes just from reading the program.

menu_000

Its return values are as follows:

▶ 3, if the user selected the "data selection" command

▶ 4, if the user selected the "graph selection" command with the D_EXIST and D_CHOSEN flags set

▶ 5, if the user selected the "view graph" command with the G_SELECTED and D_EXIST flags set

▶ 8, if the user selected the "exit program" command and `exit_program()` returned a nonzero value

menu_3

Its return values are:

▶ ESC, if the user pressed the escape key

▶ 0, if the user pressed the function F10 key

menu_005

Its return values are:

▶ 0, if the user pressed the function F10 key with the `variables_chosen` global variable set

▶ ESC, if the user pressed the escape key

▶ −1, if the user pressed the function F10 key with the `variables_chosen` global variable clear

Some more questions for the sleuth: What are the meanings of the `D_EX-IST` and `D_CHOSEN` flags and the `variables_chosen` global variable? Why does `menu_000` test flags before returning 4 or 5 when `flow_control` could test the flags before changing states? If you know the answer to the latter question, you have really begun to understand `flow_control`.

 SLEUTHING RULE 10

Investigate the variables. Determine the meanings of key variables, asking what information they carry. For global variables this may involve cross-referencing.

4.5 Conclusions

The third phase of sleuthing looks inside the modules, identifying key control structures and variables and unraveling algorithms and data structures. This phase may involve graphical aids, "copy editing," and much cross-referencing. The sleuth who is also a good programmer can best appreciate the techniques of the original programmers.

When the sleuth has developed insight into the modules, the best detective work can begin. Evidence of program transcripts can be looked at and hopefully understood.

▶▶▶▶▶ Exercises

4–1. What is the effect of the procedure `update_fields` in `MENU_003.C`?

4–2. Show that the assumption in Example 4–5 that `get_row (l_record) ≤ LR` in `update_records` is reasonable. Then explain how to simplify `update_records`' fourth IF-THEN statement under this assumption.

4–3. What are the effects of the procedures `scroll_fields_up`, `scroll_fields_down`, and `redraw_record`?

4–4. Is double-linking really necessary for variables of type `RECORD`? If so, explain why. If not, show how to implement the procedures in `RECORDS.C` with single linking.

4–5. Why is the `weight` field of the data type `RECORD` apparently unused? See `MENU_006.C` for a hint.

4–6. What is the meaning of the variable `REFRESH` in `menu_3`?

4–7. What are the meanings of the global flags `D_EXIST` and `D_CHO-SEN`? Refer to `flow_control` and `menu_3` for clues.

4–8. What are the meanings of the return values of `menu_1`, `menu_2`, `menu_004`, and `view`?

4–9. Why does `menu_000` test flags before returning 4 or 5 when `flow_control` could instead test the flags before changing states?

4–10. Sleuth the file `MENU_006.C`: Show the position of its procedures in the call graph for the Statistics/Graphics Program, discuss key control and data structures, and give a model of operation. Which of its procedures do you consider the most important?

4–11. What are the possible graphs? Sleuth the file `DISPLAY.C`, also giving attention to procedures in the files `AXIS.C`, `IGP.C`, `LOAD.C`, and `VIEWPORT.C`. Not all procedures called from `show_graph` in `DISPLAY.C` are included in the program listings, so you will have to make some hypotheses.

▶▶▶▶▶ *Problems*

4–1. Choose several procedures that you have written in various languages. For each one, draw a program graph. What kinds of structures are present in the graphs?

4–2. Investigate several alternative schemes for program specification (see the references) and illustrate their use for `MINSORT` or `MINSORT-II`.

4–3. Modify `QUADRA` to eliminate any inefficiencies you can identify, to check that A, B, and C are within the limits − 100 to 100 inclusive, as well as to check that A is positive. Draw the program graph for your modified program. Has the spaghetti gotten "thicker" or less tangled? What does this tell you about sleuthing poorly structured programs that have portions "added on" as afterthoughts?

4–4. Repeat Problem 4–3 for the program `QUADRA-II`. Is it easier to sleuth "additions" to well-structured programs?

4–5. We noted that FORTRAN is notorious for handling structures with pointers. Show how index variables can be used to facilitate pointer structures in FORTRAN, giving several examples. Contrast this with pointer usage in C.

4–6. Why is self-modifying code so dangerous and misleading to the sleuth? For what other "esoteric" features of programming must the sleuth be on the lookout?

4–7. Discuss some of the methods of error handling in the Statistics/ Graphics Program.

4–8. Records in the Statistics/Graphics Program are accessed by record number, screen, and group, but no procedure has all three as arguments. Explain why this might be so and discuss the insight it provides into the development of the Statistics/Graphics Program.

4–9. The analysis of `menu_3` was done entirely without understanding procedures such as `t_getkey`. Why was it acceptable to assume that `t_getkey` is a keyboard input function? Why type of reasoning is need here? How can the assumption be tested?

Suggested Readings

Structured programming was widely debated 20 years ago. It is well worth reading Gries's letter to the editor (1974) defining structured programming not as the absence of GOTO statements but as "the task of organizing one's thoughts in a way that leads, in a reasonable time, to an understandable expression of a computing task." Dijkstra's comments on the GOTO statement (1968) are also worth noting, as is Bohm and Jacopini's very mathematical proof (1966) that the GOTO statement is unnecessary. Some of these articles can also be found in the collections edited by Gries (1981) and by Dahl et al. (1972).

There are many graphical representations for programs, of which the flowchart is perhaps the oldest. Nassi/Shneiderman diagrams (1973) are particularly well suited to structured programming. Other graphical aids are suggested in the IEEE standards (1987) and in Martin and McClure (1985) and can be found in any software engineering text.

Among the measures of a program's complexity are McCabe's *cyclomatic complexity* metric (1976) and Halstead's *software science* metric (1977). McCabe's measures complexity of a program graph; Halstead's measures a program's "grammatical" complexity. Both have well-defined mathematical foundations. They can be found in many software engineering texts.

References

Bohm, C., and G. Jacopini. Flow diagrams, Turing machines, and languages with only two formation rules. *Communications of the ACM* 9:366–371, May 1966.

Dahl, O.-J., C. A. R. Hoare, and E. W. Dijkstra, editors. *Structured Programming.* New York: Academic Press, 1972.

Dijkstra, Edsger W. Goto statement considered harmful. *Communications of the ACM* 11:147–148, March 1968.

Gries, D., editor. *Programming Methodology.* New York: Springer-Verlag, 1981.

Gries, D. On structured programming. *Communications of the ACM* 17:655–657, November 1974.

Halstead, M. H. *Elements of Software Science.* New York: Elsevier North-Holland, 1977.

IEEE. *Software Engineering Standards.* Washington, DC: IEEE Computer Society, 1987.

Martin, James, and Carma McClure. *Diagramming Techniques for Analysts and Programmers.* Englewood Cliffs, NJ: Prentice-Hall, 1985.

McCabe, T. J. A complexity measure. *IEEE Transactions on Software Engineering* SE-2:308–320, December 1976.

Nassi, I., and B. Shneiderman. Flowchart techniques for structured programming. *ACM SIGPLAN Notices* 8:12–26, August 1973.

Testing and Transcripts: Is the Program Producing the Expected Results?

The next step in sleuthing involves looking at various program run output listings, or *transcripts*. The sleuth looks at existing transcripts to reinforce his or her mental model of the program, proposes new test cases, and compares their transcripts to what was expected, revising hypotheses as warranted.

Testing in the context of sleuthing serves a broader goal than verification of programs or searching for bugs. It serves to confirm the *internal model* of a program's behavior that the sleuth has constructed—it is primarily a verification of models and only secondarily of programs. For the sleuth, the goal of testing is not to determine whether a program is correct, but to figure out what the program does. Contrast the tasks of the software developer and the software sleuth:

▶ The developer relies on *a priori* specifications of what the program should do, whereas the sleuth relies on *a posteriori* hypotheses about what it does.

▶ The developer tests to verify that *the program's behavior is consistent with the specifications,* whereas the sleuth tests to verify that *the hypotheses are consistent with the program's behavior.*

▶ The developer seeks to *improve* the program, whereas the sleuth seeks to *understand* it.

This chapter presents four steps in testing hypotheses: determining the program's test universe; classifying test cases and prioritizing the classes in order of importance; studying test runs of the program; and finally adapting hypotheses and continuing the testing with these new hypotheses.

5.1 Determining the Test Universe

The sleuth needs to determine the program's *test universe*, the set of all valid program inputs. Understanding the universe is an important part of software sleuthing because it ensures that the sleuth knows the complete capabilities of the program—as well as the complete shortcomings. No case should be left unanalyzed.

Initially, the sleuth may not know very much about the test universe except in the most general sense. The sleuth will have to refine this knowledge as his or her understanding of the program increases.

For some programs, the test universe is fairly obvious. Consider a small subroutine that implements the three-variable Boolean NAND function. For this function the possible inputs are the eight binary triples $(0,0,0), \ldots, (1,1,1)$. For most programs, on the other hand, the test universe, even if obvious, is incredibly large and testing the program on every possible input is totally impractical. Below we show that, even under very reasonable assumptions, the MINSORT program (either version) has over 9 billion possible test cases! Even if we could run one test case every, say, 10 seconds, it would take over 2800 years to test the program. This situation with programs is more the rule than the exception.

We talk about the complete universe because it gives the sleuth an ideal framework in which to do his or her testing and transcript generation. By considering the full universe, the sleuth can get a sense of which tests increase understanding of program behavior and which tests do not.

Example 5–1

MINSORT's Test Universe

Consider again the MINSORT program (Figure 2–1), which sorts an arbitrary list of integers. (But keep in mind that, in practice, the sleuth would not know for certain exactly what MINSORT does—hence the hypothesis testing.)

Suppose the sleuth is told that in the application the list length is always a fixed integer value N, that list elements are always integers between 1 and some integer $M \geq N$, and that list elements are distinct. Thus the test universe is finite and its size equals the number of permutations of N integers between 1 and M, which is

$$M \times (M-1) \times (M-2) \times \cdots \times (M-N+1) = \frac{M!}{(M-N)!}$$

This number grows very rapidly with increasing M and N. For $N = 5$ and $M = 100$, for example, the number is $100 \times 99 \times 98 \times 97 \times 96 = 9{,}034{,}502{,}400$. In general, one might not be able to assume that the number of elements N is fixed, so the test universe would be even larger.

Example 5–2

A Triangle Classification Program and its Test Universe

Consider the program TRIANG shown in Figure 5–1 that solves the classic triangle classification problem. The problem is to determine, given A, B, and C, whether there is a triangle having sides of lengths A, B, and C, and if so, whether the triangle is equilateral (three sides equal), isosceles (two sides equal), or scalene (no sides equal).

TRIANG's test universe is the set of all triples (A, B, C). If A, B, and C are restricted to be integers between 1 and some N, then the size of the universe is

$$N \times N \times N = N^3$$

Again, the number grows very rapidly with increasing N; for $N = 100$, the number is $100^3 = 1{,}000{,}000$.

▶Figure 5–1 TRIANG Program

(a) FORTRAN version

```
PROGRAM TRIANG
TYPE *, 'ENTER A, B, C'
ACCEPT *, A, B, C
IF ((A+B.LE.C) .OR. (A+C.LE.B) .OR.
1    (B+C.LE.A)) THEN
    TYPE *, 'NOT A TRIANGLE'
ELSE
    IF ((A .EQ. B) .AND. (A .EQ. C)) THEN
        TYPE *, 'EQUILATERAL TRIANGLE'
    ELSE
        IF ((A.EQ.B) .OR. (B.EQ.C) .OR.
1           (A.EQ.C)) THEN
            TYPE *, 'ISOSCELES TRIANGLE'
        ELSE
            TYPE *, 'SCALENE TRIANGLE'
        ENDIF
    ENDIF
ENDIF
END
```

(b) C version

```
main ()
{
  float A, B, C;

  printf ("ENTER A, B, C\n");
  scanf ("%f %f %f", &A, &B, &C);

  if ((A+B <=C) || (A+C <= B) || (B+C <= A))
    printf ("NOT A TRIANGLE\n");
  else {
    if ((A == B) && (B == C))
      printf ("EQUILATERAL TRIANGLE\n");
    else {
      if ((A == B) || (B == C) || (A == C))
        printf ("ISOSCELES TRIANGLE\n");
      else
        printf ("SCALENE TRIANGLE\n");
    }
  }
}
```

Example 5–3

The Statistics/Graphics Program's Test Universe

Our model of the Statistics/Graphics Program, based on our analysis to this point, is that of a program with various states, with state transitions effected by keystrokes. The states correspond to menus and highlighted spreadsheet fields. Global flags unrelated to what is visible also affect state transitions. Our model at this point is primarily navigational; we have an idea of how to reach different parts of the program and thus how to test them. The test universe, as we understand it thus far, is the set of all sequences of keystrokes and its size in theory has no upper bound.

SLEUTHING RULE 11

Determine the test universe. In general terms, the test universe is the set of all possible inputs that may occur in the intended application environment.

5.2 Classifying Test Cases

The software sleuth can use his or her knowledge about a program's structure to extract information about the program's behavior with far fewer test cases than the theoretical maximum implied by test universe size. To see this, let us look at the test cases in the context of the program graph. Generally, every test case corresponds to a specific path in the program graph. We may consider two test cases to be equivalent, in terms of the information they give the sleuth, if their paths in the program graph are the same—that is, if they exercise the same parts of the program. (There are numerous exceptions to this, of course, but we will follow this observation for now.)

Now if the sleuth can only afford to test a program on a relative handful of test cases—as when the test universe is incredibly large—then it might not be helpful to test the program on two inputs that correspond to the same path. This is especially so for MINSORT, since MINSORT's sorting algorithm is comparative. Anything the sleuth can learn from a list corresponding to one path in MINSORT he or she can learn from any other list corresponding to that same path, because it is only the relative magnitudes of list elements that affect MINSORT's operation.

To avoid redundant tests, the sleuth must determine which tests give the same information. He or she must define classes of equivalent test cases within the test universe. From each class the sleuth can choose a representative test case, which, ideally, should give the same information as any other test case within that class, in terms of exercising the program.[1]

As a general rule, there will be far more classes of test cases than the sleuth has time or even need to test. Indeed, a handful of classes may be sufficient to meet the sleuth's goal of verifying a hypothesis about the program (as opposed to verifying the program's correctness). The sleuth must prioritize the classes by asking, "What must I understand better? What are my weakest hypotheses?"

One way to prioritize the classes is to determine their sizes, relying on the intuition that the amount of information given by a class is proportional to the number of test cases in the class. The sleuth may also focus on the cases most likely to occur in the application environment; or, the sleuth may wish to focus on the ones most difficult to understand and, consequently, most likely to lead to errors. We illustrate our point with a few examples.

---

[1]It is worth observing, however, that in choosing representatives by path, details such as procedure calls are overlooked, and it is possible that some test cases in the same class may really have a different path within the called procedure. Along the same lines, it is important to keep in mind the effect of test cases on the state of the program. Many test cases may follow the same path, but each may affect the new state and subsequent operation in a different way. In spite of these caveats, the sleuth will probably find path-based equivalence classes helpful in a first effort to exercise and understand a program.

Example 5–4

SORT's Classes of Test Cases

Consider the SORT procedure in the MINSORT program. Its program graph is shown in Figure 4–1. For the example, "input" means input to the SORT procedure, not input to the MINSORT program.

It is easy to see that if the input list is already sorted, every decision at SORT's embedded IF-THEN node will be to the right, i.e., the IF condition will not be satisfied. This means that PLACE and MIN retain the values A(I) and I throughout the Ith traversal of the outer loop. This defines one path through SORT. An input list in reverse order gives another path. For example, the list (50 40 30 20 10) gives rise to the left-right or L–R sequence

L L L L L L R R R R

as shown in the following trace through SORT:

first time through outer loop

> MIN = 50; left, MIN = 40; left, MIN = 30; left,
> MIN = 20; left, MIN = 10
> new list: 10 40 30 20 50

second time through outer loop

> MIN = 40; left, MIN = 30; left, MIN = 20; right
> new list: 10 20 30 40 50

third time through outer loop

> MIN = 30; right; right
> new list: 10 20 30 40 50

fourth time through outer loop

> MIN = 40; right
> sorted list: 10 20 30 40 50

It is not hard to see that the total number of L's and R's for a list of length N is always

$$(N-1) + (N-2) + \cdots + 1 = \frac{N(N-1)}{2}$$

since the outer loop is traversed $N-1$ times and during the Ith traversal of the outer loop $(I = 1, \ldots, N-1)$ the inner loop is traversed $N-I$ times. Each L or R corresponds to a traversal of the inner loop.

The number of different L–R sequences, then, is at most

$$2^{N(N-1)/2}$$

For $N = 5$ and $M = 100$, the number of different L–R sequences is $2^{10} = 1024$. As expected, the number is independent of M, and thus of the magnitudes of list elements.

Can all L–R sequences occur? For example, is there a list whose L–R sequence is L L L L L L L L L L? (A moment's thought will tell us "no," for to get the first four L's, the list must be in reverse order—and we already know the L–R sequence for such lists.)

Let the *shape* of an input list be the list consisting of the ranks of the input list's elements. Rank the smallest element as 1, the second smallest as 2, and so on. The shape is well defined because, as we have assumed, the elements are distinct. Written in the same order as the input list, the shape is a permutation of the list (1 2 . . . N). One can prove that two input lists have the same path through the program graph if and only if they have the same shape. Thus, for each N, there are as many realizable L–R sequences as there are permutations of (1 2 . . . N), that is, N!. For N = 5, then, there are 120 realizable sequences, in contrast to the 1024 theoretically possible L–R sequences. In other words, we can classify all test cases into N! classes.

So, by exploiting program graph structure, we have effectively reduced the size of the test universe for N = 5 and list elements between 1 and 100 from over 9 billion to only 120.

With a moment's thought it is also clear that the sizes of the classes of test cases are all the same, since each list in one class is just a permutation of a list in any other class. Thus the number of lists in each class is

$$\frac{M!}{(M-N)!\,N!}$$

For M = 100 and N = 5, the number of lists in each class is thus 100!/(95!5!) = 75,287,520.

Now suppose that all test cases are equally likely and important. Since all classes of test cases are the same size, any one class is as representative of the typical input list as any other. Sound advice for how to choose T test cases for the sorting program, then, is probably to choose one list from each of T distinct classes, if T is less than or equal to N!. When T is larger, choose more than one test case from each class, or test some other aspect of the program such as error handling.

Example 5–5

TRIANG's Classes of Test Cases

Consider the TRIANG program again. There are but four paths, and with four tests the sleuth can exercise the entire program graph. Moreover, representative test cases are very easy to derive. On the other hand, this sort of analysis says nothing of the correctness of the program—only that the different parts of the program can be exercised very easily.

The sizes of the four classes vary considerably. It is possible to prove (though we will not do so here) that of the N^3 possible triples, the breakdown into the four different path categories is given by the following expressions:

number of equilateral triangles
$$N$$

number of isosceles triangles
$$(3/4)(N-1)(3N-1), \text{ if } N \text{ is odd}$$
$$(3/4)N(3N-4), \text{ if } N \text{ is even}$$

number of scalene triangles
$$(1/4)(N-1)(N-3)(2N-1), \text{ if } N \text{ is odd}$$
$$(1/4)N(N-2)(2N-5), \text{ if } N \text{ is even}$$

number of nontriangles

$$(1/2)N(N^2 - 1)$$

Thus, if $N = 5$, there are 125 input triples of which 5 correspond to equilateral triangles, 42 to isosceles, 18 to scalene, and of which 60 are nontriangles.

Consider now, as an extreme case, that the sleuth has time for only two test cases. Not paying attention to class sizes, it is conceivable that the sleuth might test the triples (2, 2, 2) (an equilateral triangle) and (2, 5, 6) (a scalene triangle). Even if these tests gave information about all equilateral and scalene triangles (more precisely, all input triples resulting in those paths), the sleuth would still know the program's behavior for only 23 of the 125 different input triples. This is less than 20 percent of the test universe size. If information is really proportional to class size, the sleuth should choose test cases for isosceles triangles and nontriangles, for their classes cover 102 cases—over 80 percent of the test universe.

Example 5–6

The Statistics/Graphics Program's Classes

Let us look briefly at the Statistics/Graphics Program. Our initial test universe was the set of all possible sequences of keystrokes. Making the test universe manageable requires employing the concept of state. The sleuth must view the program not only as mapping sequences of input strings to sequences of output strings, but also as continually updating the program's state. This point of view can simplify sleuthing because test cases that take different paths through the program but arrive at the same state can be considered equivalent; this view can also make sleuthing very difficult because it is usually much harder to observe a program's state than to observe its input and output. Moreover, describing the state more abstractly than in terms of values of each variable can be very difficult indeed.

We can partition the test universe in a rough way according to the state—for example, menu or highlighted spreadsheet field—to which a sequence of keystrokes leads. The number of states is small and finding a representative sequence leading to a given state is not hard.

Which classes of test cases are important? One of our early goals (as previously noted in Example 3–3) was to determine the source of error in a particular call to wgetf; thus the class that exercises that call is important. A class that enters the help screen would probably be important also. Depending on what else we wanted to learn (graph selection? record sorting? statistics?), other representatives would be important, too.

SLEUTHING RULE 12

Classify test cases. Study the program graph to determine which inputs provide the same information about hypotheses. Prioritize the classes.

5.3 *Studying Program Transcripts*

Having determined which classes of test cases to test, the sleuth can profit greatly by looking at program transcripts. Good programmers usually save a variety of "hypothetical" test runs for future use, which may address some of the classes. However, the only transcripts available may be those generated during actual use of the software by its consumers. This is unfortunate in one way, since the actual data input may be very complex, and if the data is not "random," the same limited classes may always be invoked. Generally the sleuth must supplement existing transcripts with new ones of his or her own creation.

Finding a representative test case in a given class is a nontrivial practical problem that professional software engineers know all too well. They (or the sleuth) may be called upon to exercise a very specific portion of an existing program to find out why it is not working correctly. How do they steer the control flow of the program to a specific program portion? What input values will get it there?

Let us assume that the sleuth has actual access to the source program, as opposed to access only to its listings or to the executable program. If the sleuth can only run the program and not modify it to make the minor enhancements described below, the job is more difficult. For then the program is almost like the proverbial "black box" of engineering, and the sleuth can only observe what it does without the ability to "twiddle" it at all.

It is a relatively simple matter to insert simple debug statements at key places in the program to identify which procedure or statement is being executed. Often programs will already have these in the form of conditionally compiled statements. By recompiling the source program with the "debug option" activated, these statements can be automatically included in the program. Of course, the statements may not be where they are needed, so inserting additional statements at particular places of interest is probably something that has to be done anyway. Needless to say such changes should only be made to copies of the original program and should be well documented.

Most modern programming environments offer a variety of software development tools, among them the *interactive debugger* (see Appendix A). An interactive debugger lets the sleuth stop the execution of a program at a given statement, step one statement at a time, examine variable values, and the like. If a debugger is readily available and easy to use, all the better to analyze program behavior with. But if the debugger is unwieldly, it may be better to modify the program manually as described above.

Now the sleuth can try to generate the specific representative test cases needed to verify certain hypotheses about the program. We give two examples.

Example 5–7

MINSORT's Transcripts

How do we find tests that follow each specific path of the MINSORT program? The sleuth can solve this problem in a straightforward manner: Simply choose lists that are permutations of (1 . . . N). Each permutation corresponds to one class of equivalent test cases. To exercise the class of test cases with the shape (3 5 2 1 4), for example, the sleuth can simply choose the list (3 5 2 1 4). If list elements were restricted to between 101 and 200, an appropriate test list having this shape would be, among others, the list (156 187 132 107 176).

It is an interesting mathematical challenge to determine the L–R sequence corresponding to a given shape and to determine exactly which L–R sequences can occur. Toward this end, we give a modified SORT procedure in Figure 5–2 with informational debugging statements that display the L–R sequence.

▶ Figure 5–2   SORT Procedure with Informational Debugging Statements

```
C
C       SORT module  ----------------------------------
C
        SUBROUTINE SORT(A, N)
        INTEGER A(100), PLACE
C
        DO 1000 I = 1, N-1
C
        MIN = A(I)
D       TYPE *,'MIN =',MIN
        PLACE = I
C
        DO 500 J = I+1, N
C
        IF(A(J) .LT. MIN) THEN
            PLACE = J
            MIN = A(J)
D           TYPE *,'LEFT, MIN =',MIN
D       ELSE
D           TYPE *,'RIGHT'
        ENDIF
C
500     CONTINUE
C
        CALL SWAP(A(I), A(PLACE))
C
1000    CONTINUE
        RETURN
        END
C
```

Example 5–8

The Statistics/Graphics Program's Transcripts

For the Statistics/Graphics Program, one initial transcript we had was a sequence of keystrokes and data entry that led to the erroneous display related to `wgetf`. Since the Statistics/Graphics Program is interactive its transcripts are generally interactive sessions and cannot be recorded on paper (unless we choose to "capture" the session using typical terminal emulator software). In practice, these transcripts would provide much more information than the length of this example suggests.

Studying the transcript, we were able to confirm a rudimentary mental model of program behavior involving `main` calling `flow_control`, `flow_control` calling `menu_3`, and so on down to the call to the procedure `atof` whose floating-point return value was being erroneously interpreted as an integer. We not only verified our hypothesis that certain keystrokes and data entry would lead to a particular program state, but we also corrected an error.

SLEUTHING RULE 13

Gathering clues is what (classical) detection is all about. Thus the next maxim: Study program transcripts. Study existing ones if available, and create new ones for representative test cases of interest.

5.4 Adapting Hypotheses

As the sleuth learns new things about a program, his or her tests should naturally become more finely tuned and more informative. The simplest testing strategy is one that just catalogs program behavior. The sleuth simply defines a set of inputs with which to test the program using a structurally based approach in the spirit of what we have presented above. The outcomes of each test are noted but no immediate effort is undertaken to correct any hypotheses. This is the mechanism that is often used in automated testing schemes. For example, it is a simple enough matter to write a program that randomly generates 50 different lists of numbers of different shapes, invoking `MINSORT` on each list. But it is generally more informative, albeit more difficult, to employ an adaptive testing strategy.

The typical scenario is as follows: A short preset list of tests is chosen. They are carried out. If they are all consistent with hypotheses, fine. A new short list is selected, and so on. However, as soon as program behavior is inconsistent with hypotheses, including the hypothesis "unpredictable," the sleuth chooses new tests. At this point old tests have been shown to be based on a misunderstanding and may provide no meaningful information.

An adaptive scheme lets the sleuth learn much about the program—and the gaps in his or her understanding of it—in the constrained amount of time available. The fewer tests available, the more sense it makes for the sleuth to adapt hypotheses. A note of caution, however: It may not be worthwhile to adapt too frequently, and a good balance between testing and improving hypotheses is what is needed.

We conclude with an example of adaptation for the Statistics/Graphics Program.

Example 5–9

Adapting Hypotheses for the Statistics/Graphics Program

Our model of Examples 5–3, 5–6, and 5–8 is not refined enough to answer many of the questions we might ask. States based on menu or highlighted spreadsheet field alone are not sufficient. In particular, the call to `wgetf` is conditioned on more than just the user pressing the enter key with `window = 0`; it also requires the following (see Example 4–4):

▶ `rec_ptr->day_to_use` $\neq 0$

▶ `params[p].ptype = 1`

These conditions would be made clear by generating transcripts and observing that floating point values are accepted only when

▶ a file has been loaded into a record in the spreadsheet

▶ an additional column on the spreadsheet for a noncategorical parameter has been defined

These transcript-based observations lead us to refine our model. The refined model incorporates what the transcripts show, that the state of the program reflects not only menu or highlighted field, but also whether or not a file has been loaded and what kind of additional parameters have been defined. The test universe remains the same—sequences of keystrokes—but we refine our initial partition. Specifically, sequences of keystrokes that lead to the same menu but different choices such as parameters fall into different classes of test cases and we need separate representatives for these separate choices.

Our model is a bit more sophisticated now. The user is not merely navigating to different screens, but is actually making choices in those screens. However, generating transcripts would again reveal shortcomings in this improved model. In particular, the program produces graphs and statistics that depend on the nutritional data loaded into records.

A final refinement (at least for the purposes of this chapter) incorporates data into the model. When we begin to ask questions about how graphs are plotted and how statistics are computed, we realize that data values affect every aspect, from whether there are enough data to how axes are labeled. Our test universe has changed. It is no longer only sequences of keystrokes; it now includes all possible data. In fact, one might argue that the test universe is only data and that the user, rather than navigating and making choices, is analyzing data. We return to this argument in Problem 5–8. For now it is sufficient to observe that generating transcripts has led to significant refinements in our model of the program, leading to something that is quite consistent with what we expected on first reading the program's specifications: that the Statistics/Graphics Program collects, analyzes, and displays statistics on nutritional data.

SLEUTHING RULE 14

Adapt hypotheses to test results. Determine new test cases based on the revised hypotheses and continue testing.

5.5 Conclusions

The subject of software testing and its role in sleuthing is a complex, open-ended one. Only a limited number of transcripts can be examined and the sleuth must continually test and refine his or her understanding of the program. The guidelines presented here should be of help in developing the perspective needed by the sleuth in this difficult quest.

▶ ▶ ▶ ▶ ▶ Exercises

5–1. Recall that program `ORBIT` (Example 2–4) inputs an atomic number and outputs an ideal electronic configuration. If the atomic number input is assumed to be between 1 and 107, what is the size of `ORBIT`'s test universe? How many distinct program paths are there? What are the sizes of each class of equivalent test cases?

5–2. Is the L–R sequence L R L R L R L R L R realizable in `MIN-SORT`? If not, explain why not; if so, give a list that has this L–R sequence.

5–3. Verify the formulas given in Example 5–5 for the sizes of each class of test cases in the triangle classification problem. This is a nontrivial problem whose goal is to convince you of the difficulty of mathematically modeling software behavior. A good sleuth must often be a good mathematician.

5–4 Consider the C procedure shown below that determines on what day of the week a given date falls. Assume that the input is a date between March 1, 1900 and December 31, 1999. What are the classes of test cases?

```
int DateToWeekDay (Month, Day, Year)
int Month, Day, Year;
{
   int WeekDay;
```

```
if (Month <= 2) {
  Month = Month + 12;
  Year--;
}

WeekDay = 4 + (Year-1900) + (Year-1900)/4;

switch (Month) {
  case 6: case 14: WeekDay += 1; break;
  case 9: case 12: WeekDay += 2; break;
  case 4: case 7: WeekDay += 3; break;
  case 10: WeekDay += 4; break;
  case 5: case 13: WeekDay += 5; break;
  case 8: WeekDay += 6; break;
}

WeekDay += (Day - 1);

return (WeekDay % 7);
}
```

5–5. Suppose that the C procedure of Exercise 5–4 were rewritten and the switch statement replaced by a table lookup statement

```
WeekDay += MonthOffset[Month];
```

where the table is declared as

```
int MonthOffset[15] ={ 0, 0, 0, 0, 3, 5, 1,
                       3, 6, 2, 4, 0, 2,
                       5, 1 };
```

How would the classes of equivalent test cases change? What does this tell you about the influence of program data on testing?

5–6. Give an initial model of what the following FORTRAN program fragment does and describe what test cases you would need to verify your hypotheses. Make any reasonable assumptions about the test universe.

```
      J = 0
1     IF (I .EQ. 0) GOTO 3
      IF (I/2*2 .NE. I) J = 1 - J
      I = I/2
      GOTO 1
3     CONTINUE
```

5–7. Repeat Exercise 5–6 for the following program fragment.

```
      M = 0
      K = 1
```

```
1        ACCEPT *, X
         M = (1 - (1/K)) * M + (1/K) * X
         K = K + 1
         TYPE *, M
         GOTO 1
```

5-8. Repeat Exercise 5-6 for the program fragment of Exercise 1-3.

5-9. Repeat Exercise 5-6 for the program fragment of Exercise 1-4.

5-10. Some paths are hard to cover. Construct a nontrivial test case (N at least 3) that covers the CALL statement in the following FORTRAN program fragment. What is the program doing?

```
         ACCEPT *, N, (M(I, 1), I = 1, N)
         DO 10 K = 1, N
         DO 11 I = 1, N-K
         IF (M(I+1, K) .NE. M(I, K)) GOTO 12
11       CONTINUE
         GOTO 20
12       DO 13 I = 1, N-K
         M(I, K+1) = M(I+1, K) - M(I, K)
13       CONTINUE
10       CONTINUE
20       IF (K .EQ. N) CALL OUTPUT(M)
```

5-11. Repeat Exercise 5-10 for the following FORTRAN program fragment.

```
         ACCEPT *, N, (M(I), I= 1, N)
         INV = .FALSE.
         DO 10 I = 1, N
         DO 11 J = I+1, N
         IF (M(I) .GT. M(J)) INV = .NOT. INV
11       CONTINUE
10       CONTINUE
         IF (INV) CALL OUTPUT(M)
```

What is the probability that a test case selected at random covers the CALL statement? Explain.

▶▶▶▶▶ *Problems*

5-1. Find a simple program that someone else has written and for which there are transcripts of test cases. Are there any program paths that have not been followed in the existing transcripts? Make reasonable assumptions about the test universe.

5-2. Continuing Problem 5-1, determine a new test case for the program that follows one of the paths not traversed by the existing test cases (if there is one). Show how you would insert debug statements to verify that the program is indeed following the path in question.

5–3. Implement the function `ROOT` discussed in Example 4–3 in either FORTRAN or C. How big is its test universe? How many distinct program paths are there for this program? Can you estimate or calculate the sizes of each class of test cases?

5–4. Find a program that implements a nonrecursive comparative list-sorting algorithm different from that of `MINSORT`, such as a bubble sort, and repeat the analysis given in Sections 5.1 and 5.2. Specifically, calculate the test universe size, draw the program graph, and try to estimate the number of distinct program paths and the number of input lists associated with each path.

5–5. Write a program that generates the 120 distinct-shape five-element lists needed to test every realizable path of `MINSORT`. Now discuss what is involved in testing the testing program. Can you write a program that tests it?

5–6. Write a simple FORTRAN or C program that reads in a list of N integers between 0 and M and computes their mean rounded to the nearest integer. What is the size of its test universe?

5–7. Consider the program of Problem 5–6. How many distinct program paths are there? What are the sizes of the classes of equivalent test cases?

5–8. Is the "data only" model the right model for the test universe of the Statistics/Graphics Program? Explain.

5–9. Based on what you have learned thus far about the Statistics/Graphics Program, describe in general terms how you would go about testing your model.

Suggested Readings

One of the goals of the early research into the mathematical meanings of programs was to determine ways to develop correct programs without debugging into correctness (McCarthy 1963; Floyd 1967; Hoare 1969). Formal proofs of correctness are a step in this direction (Loeckx and Sieber 1987). One of the classic references in testing is a book by Myers (1979). Hetzel (1988) gives a more recent guide and a chapter or more on testing can be found in almost any software engineering text.

The triangle classification problem is from another of Myers's books (1976).

References

Floyd, R W. Assigning meanings to programs. *Proceedings of the American Mathematical Society Symposium in Applied Mathematics* 19:19–31, 1967.

Hetzel, William C. *The Complete Guide to Software Testing.* 2d ed. Wellesley, MA: QED Information Sciences, 1988.

Hoare, C. A. R. An axiomatic basis for computer programming. *Communications of the ACM* 12:576–580, 583, October 1969.

Loeckx, Jacques, and Kurt Sieber. *The Foundations of Program Verification.* 2d ed. New York: Wiley, 1987.

McCarthy, J. Towards a mathematical theory of computation. *Proceedings of the IFIP Congress.* IFIP, 1963.

Myers, Glenford J. *The Art of Software Testing.* New York: Wiley, 1979.

Myers, Glenford J. *Software Reliability.* New York: Wiley, 1976.

Improving Documentation: Writing Down What We Have Learned about the Program

Educators often say that there is no better way to consolidate understanding of a subject than to try to teach it to someone else. By analogy, the software sleuth has not completed his or her work until attempting to convey the conclusions of that work to someone else. For this will underscore what the sleuth *really* understands and what he or she just appears to understand. The vehicle for this is *documentation*.

Presumably there is already some kind of documentation for the program. But, unless the people who originally wrote it were unusually disciplined, it is probably inadequate for meeting the goals we discuss in this final chapter. The existing documentation can, however, serve as a base. Our discussion has two parts: writing a reference manual and writing a user's manual.

6.1 Writing a Reference Manual

Software development is a curious thing. Even those of us who should know better often develop algorithms and data structures to solve a problem while writing a draft of the program itself. This is analogous to designing a circuit board with a soldering iron, not a schematic. Thus the sleuth often is forced to work with programs that suffer from lack of good *specifications*. Much of modern software engineering is concerned with the issue of how to specify programs and, more importantly, what such specifications should contain. There are a variety of standard approaches to specifying algorithms. The suggested readings at the end of the chapter give more information concerning these various specification schemes.

Since the sleuth must reconstruct specifications *a posteriori*, a thorough knowledge of and experience with specification theory is essential for successful sleuthing.

The sleuth's first and key item of documentation, then, should be a reference manual that gives a complete specification of the software, complementary to the program listing itself. The reference manual should be sufficiently detailed to permit a software maintainer to take over the development and debugging of the software with minimal difficulty. It should critique the program, differentiating between how it was actually implemented and how it should have been implemented. The reference manual must leave no aspects of the program implementation unstated or unresolved.

It is not to be expected that the first draft of a reference manual will result in a finished, polished product. It may require the help of a professional manual writer to prepare it for final production. But the very exercise of writing will hone the sleuth's knowledge of the program. Should a reference manual already exist, the sleuth's course should be to rewrite the documentation in his or her own words.

We recommend that the manual consist of the following sections, in the order given:

▶ an overview of the program's purpose, organization and design; scope and limitations of the program; program specifications

▶ a somewhat more detailed view of the calling net, data structures, and algorithms

▶ a description of each procedure, including inputs, outputs, procedures it calls, procedures calling it, purpose, general algorithm, and other technical information

▶ a detailed list of all known or suspected errors in the program, along with as much information as possible about which conditions invoke those errors

▶ a summary of the known test cases for which the program has been run, along with the transcripts of such runs

Now you may say, "Why write this? No one will ever read it!" This may be true. In some sense, however, it does not matter. It is the *act* of writing it, as much as the document itself, that serves to consolidate understanding of the software. And, of course, if it is read, think of the benefits.

Example 6-1

MINSORT's Reference Manual

A reference manual for MINSORT is shown in Figure 6–1. It shows a fairly informal approach to specification. In constructing such a reference manual the sleuth must ask the following questions and hope that the answers to them have been written down *somewhere*. If not, the sleuth must answer them:

▶ What type of sorting algorithm is being used?

▶ How is the unsorted list stored? Is a copy retained? What kinds of auxiliary storage are involved?

▶ What limits are there on the lengths of the lists and on the sizes of the numbers themselves? Are all list elements to be distinct?

▶ How are error conditions (e.g., an out-of-range number, or a number of the wrong type) handled?

These questions involve four distinct issues: the algorithm, the data structures, the assumed limitations, and error handling. These issues characterize any good program development approach. If the answers to these issues are ambiguous, the sleuthing process is handicapped.

A little research into sorting algorithms (see the suggested readings) reveals that they are generally of one of two types—comparative or distributive. MINSORT's algorithm is of the first type. It involves comparing list elements against one another. Notice also that MINSORT sorts in place.

▶Figure 6–1   MINSORT's Reference Manual

MINSORT inputs a list of integers, sorts the list in increasing order by repeated selection of minimum elements, and outputs the result.

Calling Net

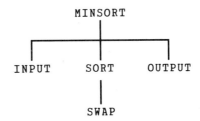

Data Structures

List is represented in two parts: an integer length (maximum 100) and an integer array of list elements. List is sorted in place.

Algorithms

Selection sort. Let N be length of the list and $A(1), \ldots, A(N)$ be the elements. There are $N–1$ iterations. During the ith iteration the minimum element among $A(i), \ldots, A(N)$ is found and exchanged with $A(i)$. After the ith iteration, $A(1), \ldots, A(i)$ are the i smallest elements in increasing order, so after the $(N-1)$st iteration the list is sorted.

Procedures

```
PROGRAM MINSORT
```

MINSORT calls INPUT to input the list, calls SORT to sort the list, and calls OUTPUT to output the sorted list.

```
SUBROUTINE INPUT(A,N)
INTEGER A(100)          ! list elements (output)
INTEGER N               ! list length (output)
```

INPUT writes a prompt to the terminal, reads the list length, reads the list elements, then writes the list elements back. Called by MINSORT.

```
SUBROUTINE OUTPUT(A,N)
INTEGER A(100)          ! list elements (input)
INTEGER N               ! list length (input)
```

OUTPUT writes the list elements to the terminal. Called by MINSORT.

```
SUBROUTINE SORT(A,N)
INTEGER A(100)          ! list elements (input/output)
INTEGER N               ! list length (input)
```

SORT sorts the list elements in increasing order by repeated selection of minimum elements, calling SWAP to exchange elements. PLACE and MIN are maintained during each iteration as the index and value of the minimum element. Called by MINSORT.

```
SUBROUTINE SWAP(X,Y)
INTEGER X,Y             ! values to exchange (input/output)
```

SWAP interchanges the values of X and Y. Called by SORT.

Limitations

Length of list is assumed to be between 1 and 100. List length is not checked by any procedure.

Error Handling

None.

Transcripts

See User's Manual.

Example 6-2

modify's Reference Manual Section

We now give a reference manual section for the procedure modify (Figure 6-2). Our description is quite detailed and more extensive than what we have already covered in Example 4-4 (indeed, it is based on some information not listed in Appendix B). The manual section discusses such issues as what `window` and `field` mean, and why the return value in one case appears to indicate an error even when an operation is successful. All these details are the result of careful sleuthing, not only of the procedure of interest but also of how it fits into the program as a whole. Such details are essential to understanding and improving the Statistics/Graphics Program.

We make a final note on the documentation: It doesn't follow the rule "leave no aspects unstated." Statements such as "in some cases" need further refinement. The manual is also missing some sections, such as the one on data structures. Consider it as a draft.

▶ Figure 6–2 modify's Reference Manual Section

Module

`modify`

File

`MENU_003.C`

Inputs

▶ `s`—screen, 0 or 1

▶ `record`—current record index

▶ `params`—additional parameter information

▶ `field`—current field

▶ `window`—current window

The last four are global variables.

Outputs

Return value is 0 if no user input is accepted, 1 if accepted and successful, −1 if input accepted and unsuccessful (but see notes below).

Calls

`category_menu, default_keys, get_record, help_off, help_on, message, perform_file_loading, process_error, quick_load, redraw_record, refresh_status_line, restore_cursor, save_cursor, select_data_file, set_flag, show_cursor, t_getkey, t_keywait, warning, wgetf, wgetl`

Called By

`menu_3`

Purpose

Modifies current field in current record of data entry screen (spreadsheet), possibly also adding new records.

Algorithm

Modifies record in one of several ways depending on the current window and field:

▶ if `window` = 0 and `field` = 0, asks user to select a data file (see `select-_data_file`), then loads that file into the current and possibly new records (see `perform_file_loading`)

▶ if `window` = 0, `field` = 1, and the current record has data, asks the user from what day in the data file to begin loading data, and loads data starting at that day into the current record

▶ if `window` ≠ 0, the current record has data, and `params[window-1 +field]` = 1, asks the user for a floating-point value and gives the selected parameter in the current record that value

▶ if `window` ≠ 0, the current record has data, and `params[window-1 +field]` ≠ 1, asks the user for an integer or asks the user to select a category from a menu (see `category_menu`), depending on whether a key is pending, and gives the parameter that value or category

Redraws the record and sets the global flag `D_MODIFY` when successful and in some cases when unsuccessful.

Error Handling

▶ generates "SELECT DATA FILE FIRST" warning when current record has no file name

▶ generates one of several messages with `process_error` when data cannot be loaded

▶ generates "VALID DAY IS 1-<days_in_file> ONLY" message when a user requests to begin loading data at a day not in the file

▶ generates "MUST BE <Min> TO <Max>" warning when user supplies a floating-point value too small or too large

▶ generates "Use keys 1 thru <ptype> to select a category for <pname>" message when user supplies an integer too small or too large

▶ generates "SELECT DATA FILE AND DAY TO USE FIRST" message when `window` > 0 and current record has neither a starting day nor a file name

▶ generates "SELECT DAY TO USE FIRST" message when `window` > 0 and current record has a file name but no starting day

Notes

`menu_3` calls `modify` when the user presses the enter key. It also calls `modify` when both (a) `window` ≠ 0 or `field` ≠ 0, and (b) the user presses , "+", "−", "." or an alphanumeric key. Except for the enter key case, `menu_3` keeps the key pressed as "typeahead," so the key is considered the first character input to the selected field.

`window` and `field` have the following meanings:

▶ `window` = 0, `field` = 0—file name field

▶ `window` = 0, `field` = 1—start day field

▶ `window` = 1,2,3, `field` = 0,1,2—additional parameters field

Windows and fields are selected with the left and right arrow keys (see `update-_fields`).

Records are selected with the home, end, up arrow, and down arrow keys (see `update_records`).

Screen 0 or 1 (the `s` argument to `modify`) is selected with the function F2 key if `gdefs.analysis > 2` (see `before_after`).

Additional parameters come in two types (see `menu_2`):

▶ `params[p].ptype = 1`—noncategorical, accepting floating-point values

▶ `params[p].ptype ≠ 1`—categorical, accepting integers 1 to `params[p].ptype` corresponding to category names

Return value is −1 when `window = 0` and `field = 0` regardless of success; this is to prevent `menu_3` from calling `advance_cursor` since `perform_file_loading` moves the cursor (the selected record) itself. Otherwise return values are as expected.

Note: This Reference Manual is greatly enhanced by suitable graphics. The reader is asked to do this as an exercise.

Example 6–3

RECORDS.C's Reference Manual Section

Our next example is a reference manual description of the file RECORDS.C (see Figure 6–3). It shows how a set of procedures can be documented together. In a sense, the set of procedures is its own "data abstraction" module. The description is deliberately abridged to refer only to procedures listed in Appendix B.

The comment on `insert_link` at the end illustrates a problem often faced by the sleuth: loose threads of program code.

▶ **Figure 6–3   RECORDS.C's Reference Manual Section**

File

`RECORDS.C`

Procedures

`add_link, get_record, get_record_count, insert_link, new_record, records_exit, release_screen, remove_blank_records, remove_link`

Inputs/Outputs

(Not including arguments to procedures)

▶ `vscreens`—linked list heads

▶ `gdefs.gcnt`—number of groups

▶ `gdefs.analysis`—type of analysis

▶ `gdefs.group`—current group

These are all global variables.

Calls

`clear_dine_arrays, cls` (i.e., `clear_screen`—see `STRUCT.H`), `free, malloc, strcpy, warning`

Called By

Procedures in `INDIVID.C`, `MAIN.C`, `MENU_000.C`, `MENU_003.C`, `MENU_006.C`.

Purpose

Procedures in `RECORDS.C` manage the storage and order of records in data entry screens. Records are organized into screens, which are organized into groups. The procedures have the following purposes (the order is logical, not alphabetical):

▶ `new_record()` allocates storage for a new record, initializes some of its fields, and returns a pointer to the record

▶ `release_screen(s)` deallocates storage for all records in screen `s` of every group

▶ `get_record(s,record)` returns a pointer to record number `record` in screen `s` of the current group

▶ `add_link(rec,screen)` and `insert_link(rec,screen)` make the record to which `rec` points the new last record in screen `screen` of the current group

▶ `get_record_count(screen)` returns the number of records in screen `screen` of the current group

▶ `remove_link(ptr,s,group)` removes the record to which `ptr` points from screen `s` of group `group` and deallocates storage for that record

▶ `remove_blank_records(screen)` removes and deallocates all records whose `day_to_use` field is 0 from screen `screen` of every group

▶ `records_exist()` returns a logical value indicating whether there are records whose `day_to_use` field is nonzero in any screen of any group

Algorithm(s)

Storage for records is allocated and deallocated with the C run-time library functions `malloc` and `free`. Records are counted, searched, and selected and new records are added by traversing a linked list. A record is removed by linking together its predecessor and successor.

Data Structures

Screens are represented as double-linked lists whose heads are stored in the two-dimensional array `vscreens` (one dimension is group, the other is screen). List links are part of the records.

Error Handling

`new_record` generates a warning "Unable to allocate memory for data record <ABORTING>" and terminates the Statistics/Graphics Program when it cannot find storage for a new record.

Notes

Record numbers start at 0.

The dimensions of `vscreens` are 5 and 2 (see `EXTERN.H` and `STRUCT.H`). There can be at most five groups and two screens in a group.

The number of meaningful groups is stored in `gdefs.gcnt`. The number of meaningful screens in a group is either one or two, depending on `gdefs.analysis`:

▶ 1—individual analysis (one group, one screen)

▶ 2—single group analysis (one group, one screen)

▶ 3—single group before/after intervention (one group, two screens)

▶ 4—multiple groups before/after intervention (one to five groups, two screens/group)

`change_groups` in `MENU_003.C` updates `gdefs.group`.

`new_record` initializes fields of a record as follows (also see `clear_dine_array` in `IO.C`):

▶ `filename`—null string

▶ `individual`—null string

▶ `version`—0

▶ `day_to_use`—0

▶ `days_in_file`—0

▶ `weight`—(not initialized)

▶ `actual`—first `FPM` elements to 0, otherwise to `Unknown`

▶ `low`—all elements to `Unknown`

▶ `high`—all elements to `Unknown`

▶ `date`—null string

▶ `next`—null pointer

▶ `prev`—null pointer

Other procedures access the fields, including those in `IO.C`, `LOAD.C`, `MENU_003.C`, and `MENU_006.C`. Several procedures outside `RECORDS.C` traverse the linked lists, including `load_array` in `LOAD.C`.

`add_link` and `insert_link` are identical but it is not clear why; it seems reasonable that `insert_link` should place a record between two records that are not at the end of the linked list, but it does not. `insert_link` is never called in the Statistics/Graphics Program.

Example 6–4

An Overview of the Statistics/Graphics Program

We conclude with an overview of the Statistics/Graphics Program (Figure 6–4). With it, the "case is closed," as far as reference manuals are concerned. Again we note that the description refers only to the procedures listed in Appendix B.

▶ Figure 6–4   Reference Manual Overview
of the Statistics/Graphics Program

The Statistics/Graphics Program consists of over 126 procedures, not counting the procedures they call in standard and custom libraries. The procedures fall generally into four categories (which correspond to the top-level directory and three subdirectories in which files are stored):

▶ top-level—main program, initialization, common utilities

▶ \MENUS—user interface for all display screens except graphics

▶ \GRAPHS—user interface for graphics, statistics

▶ \RECORDS—I/O, data management

Modularization is primarily functional; each program display screen and operation has its own procedure. There is some data-oriented modularization for data management and graphics. Data structures are relatively simple; control structures are somewhat complex.

The most important files as far as high-level understanding of the program is concerned are MENU_003.C, FLOW.C, and DISPLAY.C and within them the most important procedures are menu_3, flow_control, and view. The most important files for low-level understanding are RECORDS.C and VIEWPORT.C.

SLEUTHING RULE 15

Write a reference manual. Reconstruct the program's specifications and implementation details. Be a reverse engineer.

6.2 Writing a User's Manual

Contrasted with the reference manual is the second item of documentation: the *user's manual*. Whereas the goal of the reference manual is to document the details of the program itself, the goal of the user's manual is to teach. It is designed for the potential and current users of the software. It contains, among other things:

▶ a description of the intended application of the software

▶ instructions on how to run the program, how to specify its inputs, and how to interpret its outputs

▶ typical transcripts of the program

▶ limitations and known error conditions

▶ a summary of the user interface, including all error messages

Just as the reference manual can be divided into sections by procedure, the user's manual can be divided into sections by user-visible parts of a program. Often a user-visible feature described in the user's manual will correspond directly to one or more procedures in the reference manual.

Here we can make an analogy with a VCR. The reference manual for a VCR is the detailed technical information and data sheets needed by the technician who maintains and repairs the VCR; the user's manual is the booklet written for the consumer that describes how to use the VCR, not how to dismantle it. Thus, in the programming environment, the user's manual summarizes the program from the consumer's point of view, focusing on inputs and outputs, not internal structure.

We illustrate the second item of documentation with two examples: MINSORT and data entry in the Statistics/Graphics Program.

Example 6–5

MINSORT's User's Manual

A user's manual for MINSORT is shown in Figure 6–5. Notice the significant differences between this and the reference manual—the tutorial nature of the former, the detail of the latter. Each has its intended audience and each is important.

▶ Figure 6–5 MINSORT's User's Manual

MINSORT is a simple sorting program for lists of up to 100 numbers. You enter the length first, then the numbers one after another. Then MINSORT displays the original list, sorts the list, and displays the sorted list, starting with the smallest number.

The length of your list must be between 1 and 100. Be sure to enter only integers for the length and the numbers in your list. You can enter the numbers on one or more lines. Separate numbers with commas or spaces. List numbers can be positive, negative, or zero but must be between the limits set by your computer.

In the following transcript the five-number list (56 87 32 07 76) is sorted. User input is underlined and the system prompt is "$":

```
$ run minsort
please enter list to be sorted
enter length of list, then list
5
56 87 32 07 76
original list is          56        87
32        07        76
sorted list is           07        32        56
76        87
$
```

Example 6-6

A Section of the Statistics/Graphics Program's User's Manual

We give a section of a user's manual for the Statistics/Graphics Program (not necessarily the one published by DineSystems, Inc.). The section is shown in Figure 6–6. A complete user's manual would describe more fully the intended application environment, how to run the program, and so on. The section we give focuses on user interface and error handling.

▶ Figure 6–6   User's Manual Description of Data Entry

You can load data from a new file into any record. You can change the day starting at which data are loaded and the values of additional parameters in any record not labeled "PUSH ENTER" in the file name field.

To load data from a new file into a record, select the file name field and press the enter key. The program will list files with the **DNE** extension; select a file. The program will list days in the file; select one or all. Data will be loaded from the file into the record starting at the day you select and, if you select more than one day, into subsequent records.

To load data starting at a new day, select the start day field and press the enter key. Type the number of the new day and press the enter key again. Data will be loaded from the file into the record starting at the day you select. You can also just type the number and press the enter key; the initial "enter" is not necessary.

To change the value of a categorical parameter (see the section "Defining categorical parameters"), select the parameter field and press the enter key. The program will list the categories; select one.

To change the value of a noncategorical parameter, select the parameter field, press the enter key, type the new value, and press the enter key again. The value should be a real number and may include a sign (" + " or " − "), an integer part, and a fractional part preceded by a decimal point. You can also just type the value and press the enter key; the initial "enter" is not necessary.

You might encounter one of the following error messages while entering data:

▶ "SELECT DATA FILE FIRST"—when you select the start day field and press enter in a record labeled "PUSH ENTER"

▶ "VALID DAY IS 1-<days_in_file> ONLY"—when you try to load data starting at a day not in the file

▶ "MUST BE <Min> TO <Max>"—when you supply a floating-point value that is too small or too large

▶ "Use keys 1 thru <ptype> to select a category for <pname>"—when you supply a category number that is out of range

▶ "SELECT DATA FILE AND DAY TO USE FIRST"—when you attempt to change a parameter in a record labeled "PUSH ENTER"

You will also encounter an error message if the data file you try to load does not contain DINE nutritional data.

It is worthwhile to compare the set of error messages in the user's manual section with those in the reference manual description of modify (Figure 6–2). One message listed in the reference manual is not listed in the user's manual. Further sleuthing shows that the conditions in modify leading to the message can never all be satisfied at the same time. Thus the user need not be aware of the message. The observation about the error message would probably make a nice comment in a revised version of the reference manual for modify.

SLEUTHING RULE 16

Write a user's manual telling how to use the program. Put your understanding of the program into words.

6.3 *Conclusions*

The successful sleuth is a writer as well as a detective. Note how iterative sleuthing really is. The manuals described for the Statistics/Graphics Program "integrate" concepts together. This makes it worthwhile to examine the entire program again, to produce better documentation, and so on. Documentation is often a tedious process, requiring tremendous self-discipline on the part of the sleuth. But it is what separates the effective sleuth from the ineffective one, and its importance should never be minimized.

▶▶▶▶▶ *Exercises*

6–1. Write reference and user's manuals for the QUADRA program (either version) of Example 4–3.

6–2. Write a reference manual description of the following procedures in the Statistics/Graphics Program:

    a. `menu_∃`

    b. `update_records`

    c. `flow_control`

6–3. Write a user's manual description of the part of the Statistics/ Graphics Program implemented by one of the procedures in Exercise 6–2. (This is a hard one.)

6–4. Complement the reference manual for `modify` by including graphical aids (flowcharts, calling nets, state diagrams, etc.). What kinds of graphical aids work best here?

▶ ▶ ▶ ▶ ▶ *Problems*

6–1. Write (or improve) the documentation for a program you are currently using and to whose source listings you have access.

6–2. Investigate several alternative schemes for program specification (see the suggested readings) and illustrate their use for the `MIN-SORT` program.

6–3. How has the five-part approach to sleuthing presented in Chapters 2–6 helped you understand the Statistics/Graphics Program? How do you think you would approach the program if it were your job to *really* understand it?

6–4. We presented a "draft" of the reference manual for `modify`. Fill in the missing details.

Suggested Readings

Good documentation is an art as well as a science. As far as scientific references, Gehani and McGettrick (1986) provide a nice though dated collection on requirements and techniques, particular approaches, case studies, and specification systems. Almost any software engineering text has something to say on the topic. How formal we should make a specification is a topic of great interest. Liskov and Zilles (1974), for example, show how completely mathematical specifications could make it possible to prove that a program is correct. Naur (1982) argues that natural language specifications are just as useful to software developers and far easier to write.

Some of the more artistic references can be found in Brockmann (1986), Foehr and Cross (1986), Houghton-Alico (1985), and Price (1984).

For more information on sorting algorithms see any of the texts on algorithms and data structures, especially Knuth's (1981).

References

Brockmann, R. J. *Writing Better Computer User Documentation: From Paper to On-line*. New York: Wiley, 1986.

Foehr, Theresa, and Thomas B. Cross. *The Soft Side of Software: A Management Approach to Computer Documentation*. New York: Wiley, 1986.

Gehani, N. and A. D. McGettrick, editors. *Software Specification Techniques*. Reading, MA: Addison-Wesley, 1986.

Houghton-Alico, Doann. *Creating Computer Software User Guides*. New York: McGraw-Hill, 1985.

Knuth, Donald E. *Seminumerical Algorithms*. Vol. 2 of *The Art of Computer Programming*. 2d ed. Reading, MA: Addison-Wesley, 1981.

Liskov, B., and S. Zilles. Programming with abstract data types. *ACM SIGPLAN Notices* 9:50–60, April 1974.

Naur, P. Formalization in program development. *BIT* 22:437–453, 1982.

Price, Jonathan. *How to Write a Computer Manual*. Menlo Park, CA: Benjamin-/Cummings, 1984.

A

Tools for Sleuthing:
A Brief Glossary

Today's software sleuth has available a variety of tools that can aid in the sleuthing process. The experienced sleuth will use these tools much as an experienced craftsman chooses the right tool for the right job. For relatively short programs the sleuth may deal with things manually, constructing calling nets and making notes by hand. For larger, more complex programs, however, the sleuth may profit by using one or more of the bookkeeping tools described below.

In the brief glossary that follows we delineate tools by what they are *designed* to do, not by product or vendor name. This is analogous to talking about screwdrivers, saws, hammers, and so on, but not talking about a specific toolkit that may be for sale at a hardware store. The list below is not intended to be complete, but rather representative of the common types of software sleuthing tools available today.

archiver   A program to save and restore old versions of programs. This is useful in sleuthing bugs arising from program modifications.

attribute mapper   A program that lists the attributes of each identifier or other object of interest. This allows the sleuth to understand data structures and argument passing and typing more easily.

configuration controller   A program that manages multiple versions of a single module to ensure that the correct versions of the program and documentation are used. This gives the sleuth confidence that he or she is sleuthing the right version of the program.

cross-reference mapper   A program that lists the location of each reference to an identifier or other object. This is invaluable in constructing a calling net for a program.

decompiler (disassembler)   A program that maps object code back into source program statements. This is very useful for sleuthing programs in assembly language or microcode.

execution profiler   A program that determines the number of times some unit of a program, such as a statement, path, or procedure, was executed on a particular run of the program. This is useful for sleuthing path coverage, for example.

flowchart generator   A program that draws a flowchart of a source program. A tool of generally limited utility, it can be useful, nonetheless, in giving the sleuth an overview of key algorithm decisions and procedure calls.

interactive debugger   A program that facilitates examination and reinitialization of program data structures from an interactive terminal. This is an invaluable tool for the sleuth, allowing program execution to be "slowed down" enough to be examined and modified.

interface checker   A program that checks whether the interfaces of separately compiled procedures are consistent. This is a useful tool for sleuthing errors that appear to be propagated between procedures.

metric reporter   A program that examines another program with respect to a specified metric (e.g., complexity of control flow) and reports the measured value of that metric. This is useful in allowing the sleuth to concentrate on the more complex parts of programs, sections where sleuthing is usually most needed.

pretty printer   A program that reformats a program with readable indentation and spacing. Anyone who has tried to sleuth languages like C without proper indentation can certainly understand the value of this tool.

proof generator   A program that automatically or semiautomatically generates a proof of a program's correctness from its source text. This esoteric tool can be useful to the sleuth in drawing out suspect areas of a program.

standards checker   A program that detects and reports violations of programming standards. This allows the sleuth insight into the quality of the programming and the difficulty of the sleuthing job ahead.

static analyzer   A program that detects control flow anomalies such as unreachable statements and reports questionable practices such as the comparison of two real numbers for equality. This is particularly useful in sleuthing programming errors.

test-data generator   A program that generates test data that meet specified properties such as causing a particular path to be executed. Obviously, this expedites the testing process.

test harness   A program that supports easy execution of a collection of modules using specified input data. This is useful for effecting the tests that a good sleuth must undertake.

tracer   A program that reports specified events in the execution of another program. This can help the sleuth feel confident about the program flow model he or she has developed.

APPENDIX B

Statistics/Graphics Program Listings

Following are listings of a subset of the Statistics/Graphics Program. The listings include 18 `.C` files and two `.H` files, which are organized into a root directory and three subdirectories as noted:

`\GRAPHS\AXIS.C`

`\GRAPHS\DISPLAY.C`

`\MENUS\FLOW.C`

`\GRAPHS\IGP.C` (partial listing)

`\GRAPHS\INDIVID.C` (partial listing)

`\RECORDS\IO.C` (partial listing)

`\RECORDS\LOAD.C`

`\MAIN.C`

`\MENUS\MENU_000.C`

`\MENUS\MENU_001.C`

`\MENUS\MENU_002.C` (partial listing)

`\MENUS\MENU_003.C`

`\MENUS\MENU_004.C`

`\MENUS\MENU_005.C` (partial listing)

`\MENUS\MENU_006.C`

`\RECORDS\RECORDS.C`

`\GRAPHS\STATS.C`

`\GRAPHS\VIEWPORT.C`

`\EXTERN.H`

`\STRUCT.H`

```
AXIS.C

#include <stdio.h>
#include <stdlib.h>
#include <string.h>
#include <varargs.h>
#include "..\struct.h"
#include "..\extern.h"
#include "..\dinescor.h"
#include "..\graph.h"

#define DOWN 0
#define UP 1

/* 88/03/17 (BK)   Center a message at the bottom of the screen. */
display_message (va_alist)
va_dcl
{ char *mess, buff[81];
  va_list arg_ptr;

  va_start (arg_ptr);
  mess = va_arg (arg_ptr, char *);
  vsprintf (buff, mess, arg_ptr);
  va_end (arg_ptr);

  g_centers (0, buff, YMAX-spacing.ch.vgap, 0, XMAX, 0, gclr[1]);

}

display_title(va_alist)
va_dcl
{
  char  *mess, buff[81];
, va_list     arg_ptr;

  va_start(arg_ptr);
  mess = va_arg (arg_ptr, char *);
  vsprintf (buff,mess, arg_ptr);
  va_end  (arg_ptr);

  grrtulc(0, 0, XMAX, YMAX, gclr[0]);  /* Clear the region */
  g_centers(0,buff, margin.u - spacing.ch.v, margin.l,XMAX- margin.r, 0, gclr[1]);
}

/*------------------------------------------round-----------------------------*
```

```c
* Round value to increment, UP or DOWN depending on displacement.
*
* 88/02/22 (BK)   Corrected rounding of negative numbers.
*-------------------------------------------------------------------*/
int round(int value, int increment, int displacement)
{ int multiplier;

    if (increment <= 0) return (value);

    if (value > 0)
    { multiplier = value / increment;
      if (value % increment && displacement == UP) multiplier++;
      return(multiplier * increment);
    }
    else
    { multiplier = (-value) / increment;
      if (value % increment && displacement == DOWN) multiplier++;
      return(-multiplier * increment);
    }
}

static int incs[] = {1, 2, 5, 10, 20, 50, 100, 200, 500, 1000, 2000, 32000};

/*-------------------------------load_labels-------------------------*
 * Calculates evenly-spaced set of labels for range between low and
 * high. (Increment is rounded and 0, if in range, is labeled.)
 * Does not exceed cnt labels. Returns values in labels array;
 * updates low, high and cnt. Returns increment.
 *
 * Requires: *cnt >= 3, *low <= *high.
 *
 * 88/03/07 (BK)   Completely rewritten.
 *-------------------------------------------------------------------*/

int load_labels(int *low, int *high, int *cnt, int labels[])
{ int ilow, ihigh, inc, i;
  float fcnt;

    if (*low == *high) { if (*low > Min) (*low)--; if (*high < Max) (*high)++; }

    i = 0;
    do
    { inc = incs[i];
      ilow = round(*low, inc, DOWN);
      ihigh = round(*high, inc, UP);
      fcnt = (float) (ihigh/inc) - (float) (ilow/inc) + 1.;
    }
```

```c
    while (fcnt > (float) *cnt && ++i < dim(incs));

    for (i = 0; i < (int) fcnt; i++) labels[i] = ilow + i*inc;

    *low = ilow; *high = ihigh; *cnt = (int) fcnt; return(inc);

}

/*--------------------load_ordinal_labels------------------------*
* Calculates nicely-spaced set of labels for range between low and
* high. Increment is positive but not fixed. Does not update low and
* high. Uses exactly cnt labels. Returns values in labels array.
*--------------------------------------------------------------*/

load_ordinal_labels(int low, int high, int cnt, int labels[])
{ int i;
    /* First and last points are always labeled; other points are
        labeled proportionately. */
    labels[0] = low;
    labels[cnt-1] = high;
    for (i = 1; i < cnt-1; i++)
        labels[i] = (int) ((float) ((cnt-1-i)*labels[0] + i*labels[cnt-1])
                    / (float) (cnt-1) + .5);
}

/*----------------------------plot_y_axis------------------------*
*--------------------------------------------------------------*/

plot_y_axis(int *ylow, int *yhigh, char *label, int grid)
{
    int labels[50], cnt, i, inc;
    char buff[15];
    int sx, sy;

    cnt = (YMAX - margin.d - margin.u) / VSPACING;
    if (cnt > 50) cnt = 50;
    if (cnt < 3) cnt = 3;
    inc = load_labels(ylow, yhigh, &cnt, labels);

    if (inc == -1) return(0);

    set_viewport(1, 0, margin.l, YMAX - margin.d, margin.u);
    set_window (1, 0.0, 7.0, (float) *ylow, (float) *yhigh);
    set_window_viewport(1);
```

```c
    /* Draw the y axis */
    grline(margin.l, margin.u, margin.l, YMAX - margin.d, gclr[2]);
    world_to_screen(1, 0.0, (float) *yhigh, &sx, &sy);
    g_centers(0, label, sx, margin.u, YMAX-margin.d, 2, gclr[1]);

    for (i = 0; i < cnt; i++)
    {   world_to_screen(1, 5.0, (float) labels[i], &sx, &sy);
        itoa(labels[i], buff, 10);
        strrev(buff);
        fontsprt (0, buff, sx, sy+spacing.ch.v/2, 1, gclr[1], 0);
        world_to_screen(1, 6.5, (float) labels[i], &sx, &sy);
        if (grid) grline(sx, sy, XMAX - margin.r, sy, gclr[2]);
        else grline(sx, sy, margin.l, sy, gclr[2]);
    }
}

/*---------------------------------ordinal_x axis----------------------------*
 * Labels X axis from 1 to npoints with as many numeric labels as
 * will fit. Displays axis label and optional grid lines.
 *
 * 88/02/18  (BK)  Reimplemented specifically for line graph.
 * 88/03/17  (BK)  Moved x-axis label closer to axis line.
 *---------------------------------------------------------------------------*/

ordinal_x_axis(npoints, label, grid)
int npoints, grid;
char *label;
{
    int cpl,        /* Characters per line */
        lpl,        /* Labels per line */
        labels[50], cnt, i;

    int sx, sy;
    char buff[3];

    if (spacing.ch.h == 0) spacing.ch.h = 1;
    cpl = (XMAX-margin.l-margin.r) / spacing.ch.h;

    if (npoints < 10) lpl = cpl/2 + 1;
    else if (npoints < 100) lpl = cpl/3 + 1;
    else return;

    cnt = min(lpl, npoints);
    if (cnt > 50) cnt = 50;
    if (cnt < 2) cnt = 2;

    load_ordinal_labels(1, npoints, cnt, labels);
```

```c
set_viewport(2, margin.l, XMAX - margin.r, YMAX, YMAX - margin.d);
set_window   (2, w[0].x.min, w[0].x.max, 0.0, 3.5);
set_window_viewport(2);

/* Draw the x axis */
grline(margin.l, YMAX - margin.d, XMAX - margin.r, YMAX - margin.d, gclr[2]);
world_to_screen(2, 0.0,  /* 0.25 */ 1.25, &sx, &sy);
g_centers(0, label, sy, margin.l, XMAX-margin.r, 0, gclr[1]);

/* Draw the labels */
for (i = 0; i < cnt; i++)
{ world_to_screen(2, (float) labels[i], 2.0, &sx, &sy);
  itoa(labels[i], buff, 10);
  sx -= (strlen(buff) * spacing.ch.h) / 2;
  fontsprt (0, buff, sx, sy, 0, gclr[1], 0);
}

/* Draw the tick marks (grid lines) */
for (i = 1; i <= npoints; i++)
{ world_to_screen(2, (float) i, 3.25, &sx, &sy);
  if (grid) grline(sx, sy, sx, margin.u, gclr[2]);
  else grline(sx, sy, sx, YMAX - margin.d, gclr[2]);
}

}
/* 88/03/08 (BK)   Removed staggering. */
/* 88/03/17 (BK)   Moved x-axis label closer to axis line. */
plot_x_axis3(xlow, xhigh, label, grid)
int *xlow, *xhigh, grid;
char *label;
{
  int cpl,      /* Characters per line */
      lpl,      /* Labels per line */
      labels[50], cnt, i, last_ch_x = 0;
  char buff[15];
  int sx, sy; float alt, range;

  cpl = (XMAX - margin.l - margin.r) / spacing.ch.h;

  itoa(*xhigh, buff, 10); i = max(strlen(buff), 0);
  itoa(*xlow, buff, 10); i = max(i, max(strlen(buff), 0));
  lpl = cpl / (i+1);

  cnt = lpl;
  if (cnt > 50) cnt = 50;
  if (cnt < 3)  cnt = 3;
  load_labels(xlow, xhigh, &cnt, labels);
```

```
set_viewport (2, margin.l, XMAX - margin.r, YMAX, YMAX - margin.d);
set_window   (2, (float) *xlow, (float) *xhigh, 0.0, 3.5);
set_window_viewport (2);

/* Draw the x axis */
grline(margin.l, YMAX - margin.d, XMAX - margin.r, YMAX - margin.d, gclr[2]);
world_to_screen(2, 0.0, /* 0.25 */ 1.25, &sx, &sy);
g_centers(0, label, sy, margin.l, XMAX-margin.r, 0, gclr[1]);

/* Draw the labels */
for (i = 0; i < cnt; i++)
{ world_to_screen(2, (float) labels[i], 2.0, &sx, &sy);
  itoa(labels[i], buff, 10);
  sx -= (strlen(buff) * spacing.ch.h) / 2;
  fontsprt (0, buff, sx, sy, 0, gclr[1], 0);
  world_to_screen(2, (float) labels[i], 3.25, &sx, &sy);
  if (grid) grline(sx, margin.u, sx, sy, gclr[2]);
  else grline(sx, sy, sx, YMAX - margin.d, gclr[2]);
}
```
}

DISPLAY.C

```c
#include <stdio.h>
#include <stdlib.h>
#include <search.h>
#include <string.h>
#include <varargs.h>
#include "..\struct.h"
#include "..\extern.h"
#include "..\dinescor.h"
#include "..\graph.h"

float dvalue[6][50];        /* Actual data value in input order */
float *dptr[6][50];         /* Pointers to sorted data values */
int   npoints[6];           /* Number of points */

struct Margin margin;
struct Spacing spacing;

char horizontal_axis[41];
char vertical_axis[41];

#define trunc(x)        (float) (int) x

/* Inquire whether to print the graph or not */
static int chart_size;
dump_screen()
{
    int c;
    if (graph_inquire(2))
    {
        c = get_chart_size();
        if (c == ESC)
            return (0);
        else
        {
            chart_size = c;
            return(1);
        }
    }
    else
        return(0);
}

/* Print the graph to the printer */
```

```
/* 88/03/09 (BK)  Unget F9 key if unsuccessful; added header. */

static char header[5][3][25] =
{ { "", "DineSystems, Inc.", "" },
  { "", "2211 Main St, Bldg. B", "" },
  { "", "Buffalo, NY  14214", "" },
  { "", "(716) 834-DINE, 688-2492", "" },
  { "", "" } };

static char *analysis_types[4] =
{ "individual", "single group", "single group", "multiple group" };

print_graph()
{
    char buff[BUFSIZ];
    int status, i;

    /* Check if printer ok */
    if (printer_status (0, buff, &status) == 0)
    {
        /* Construct header.  Left column gets group names, right column gets
           analysis type. */
        for (i = 0; i < 5; i++)
        { strcpy (header[i][0], ""); strcpy (header[i][2], ""); }
        for (i = 0; i < gdefs.gcnt; i++)
            strcpy (header[i][0], gdefs.group_name[i]);
        strcpy (header[0][2], analysis_types[gdefs.analysis]);
        if (gdefs.analysis == 2 || gdefs.analysis == 3)
        { strcpy (header[1][2], "(before/after)"); }
        if (gdefs.three_day) strcpy (header[2][2], "three-day");
        if (!gdefs.three_day) strcpy (header[2][2], "single-day");
        strcpy (header[3][3], "analysis");

        /* Output header to printer, then output screen. */
        for (i = 0; i < 5; i++)
            fprintf (stdprn, "\n%-28s\t%-28s\t%s",
                     header[i][0], header[i][1], header[i][2]);

        fprintf (stdprn, "\n");
        if (scrndump (display_dev.printer, 1, chart_size, 0, 0, 0, 1) != 0)
            return (0);
        fprintf (stdprn, "\f");
        return (1);
    }
    else
    {
        grrtulc(0, 0, XMAX, YMAX, gclr[0]);           /* Clear the screen */
```

```
    g_centers(0, buff, YMAX/2, 0, XMAX, 0, gclr[1]);
    g_centers(0, "Press any key to continue", YMAX-16, 0, XMAX, 0, gclr[1]);
    t_getkey();
    t_ungetkey(F_9);
    return(0);
}

/*------------------------------VIEW------------------------------*
 * User interface module for graphing.
 * PgUp sequences backward, PgDn forward. Wraparound except for
 * nutrient.breakdown. ESC, F10 exit. F5, F6 toggle options.
 * F7, F8 set y, x ranges. F9 prints.
 *
 * 88/02/03  (BK)   Reversed roles of PgUp, PgDn; corrected
 *                  end handling for type 5 (nutrient breakdown).
 * 88/03/15  (BK)   Return if unable to initialize graphics.
 * 88/03/17  (BK)   Added F4 function key (display test statistic).
 * 88/03/24  (BK)   Redisplay only for active function keys.
 *--------------------------------------------------------------- */

int view(void)
{
    int    chart = 0, stat_flag = 0, rec_flag = 0, grid_flag = 0;
    int    ret_val = 0, redisplay;
    int    invalid_key, key, i, flags, rflag;

    rec_flag = grid_flag = chart = 0;

    /* Skip invalid chart selections */
    if (gdefs.plot != 5)
    {
        while (gdefs.graphs.type[chart][Y] == -1)
        {
            chart++;
            if (chart == 5) break;
        }
        if (chart == 5)
        {
            warning("Incomplete chart selection");
            return(0);
        }
    }

    redisplay = 1;
    if (init_graphics() == -1) return(0);
```

```c
flags = 3;          /* Default */
while ( ret_val == 0)
    {
    for(i=0; i<6; i++)  npoints[i] = 0;      /* Clear arrays */
    if (stat_flag) flags |= 8; else flags &= ~8;
    if (rec_flag) flags |= 16; else flags &= ~16;
    if (grid_flag) flags |= 32; else flags &= ~32;

/* Show chart if redisplay flag set during last pass. Error conditions:
    rflag = -1 indicates not enough points; output error message
    rflag = -5 indicates graph not found, only occurs in plot 5;
             try again with old graph (hold at end)
*/
    if (redisplay) rflag = show_graph(chart, flags);
    redisplay = 0;
    if (rflag == -1) graph_message(-1);
    if (rflag == -5 && gdefs.plot == 5) rflag = show_graph(--chart, flags);

    invalid_key = 1;                /* A valid key has not been pressed */
    while(invalid_key)
        {
        invalid_key = 0;            /* Assume a valid key */
        redisplay = 0;              /* Do not refresh graphs by default */
        flags &= ~4;                /* Do not print the graph */
        switch(t_getkey())
            {
            case F_1 :  restore_graphics();
                        help(7,0);
                        init_graphics();
                        flags = 3;
                        redisplay = 1;
                        break;

            case PgDn: chart++;
                       if (gdefs.plot != 5)
                           {
                           if (chart > 4) chart = 0;
                           while (gdefs.graphs.type[chart][Y] == -1)
                               {
                               chart++;
                               if (chart > 4) chart = 0;
                               }
                           }
                       flags = 3;   /* Reset the flags */
                       redisplay = 1;
                       break;

            case PgUp: chart--;
```

```
            if (gdefs.plot != 5)
               {
               if (chart < 0) chart = 4;
               while (gdefs.graphs.type[chart] [Y] == -1)
                  {
                  chart--;
                  if (chart < 0)  chart = 4;
                  }
               }
            else if (chart < 0) chart = 0;
            flags = 3;  /* Reset the flags */
            redisplay = 1;
            break;
  case ESC : ret_val = ESC;
            break;
  case F_10: ret_val = 1;
            break;
  case F_4 : if (rflag & 8)
            { stat_flag = (stat_flag) ? 0 : 1; redisplay = 1; }
            break;
  case F_5 : if (rflag & 16)
            { rec_flag = (rec_flag) ? 0 : 1; redisplay = 1; }
            break;
  case F_6 : if (rflag & 32)
            { grid_flag = (grid_flag) ? 0 : 1; redisplay = 1; }
            break;
  case F_7 : if (rflag & 1)
            { if (get_user_y_range() == 3) flags &= ~1;
              redisplay = 1; }
            break;
  case F_8 : if (rflag & 2)
            { if (get_user_x_range() == 3) flags &= ~2;
              redisplay = 1; }
            break;
  case F_9 : if (dump_screen())
            flags |= 4;
            redisplay = 1;
            break;
  default  : invalid_key = 1;
            break;
         }
      }
   restore_graphics();
   return(0);
```

```
}

/*
 * Initialize the graphics package, margins and XMAX,YMAX and
 * put the display device in the correct graphics mode
 * All information is pulled from the configuration
 */
init_graphics()
{
    static int loaded = 0;
    int c, h, ch, lf;
    easyinit();
    if (display_dev.device == EGA && display_dev.graphics.mode >= 13)
    {
        if (fontld(0,"MONO.FY") == 0)            /* Load the IBMROM Font */
            fontld(0,"IBMROM");
    }
    else
        fontld(0,"IBMROM");                       /* Load the IBMROM Font */
    fontchg (0, -1, -1, -1, 2);
    fontinfo (0, &c, &h, &spacing.ch.hgap, &spacing.ch.vgap,
                 &spacing.ch.v, &spacing.ch.h);

    if (spacing.ch.hgap < 1) spacing.ch.hgap = 1;
    if (spacing.ch.vgap < 1) spacing.ch.vgap = 1;
    if (spacing.ch.h < 1) spacing.ch.h = 1;
    if (spacing.ch.v < 1) spacing.ch.v = 1;

    htdefind(0,gclr[0],1);
    htdefstl(0,4,1,1);

    htdefind(1,gclr[0],1);
    htdefstl(1,4,1,1);

    switch(display_dev.device)
    {
        case CGA : setibm();
            break;
        case EGA : if (display_dev.graphics.mode < 13)
                       setibm();
                   else
                       setega();
            break;
        case HGA : setherc(2);               /* Hercules Full Mode */
            break;
        case ATT : if (display_dev.graphics.mode <= 6)
```

```c
                setibm();
            else
                setatt();      /* Set up for AT&T graphics adapter */
            break;
    case TEC : settec();       /* Set up the TEMCAR graphics adapter */
            break;
    case MGA : warning("Can't display graphs on this device");
            return(-1);
            break;
    default:  warning("Device unsupported or not configured");
            return(-1);
            break;

    }

    initgraf(display_dev.graphics.mode, 1, 1);

    /* Hard code the margins */
    margin.l = 48; margin.r = 36; margin.u = 16; margin.d = 36;

    XMAX = display_dev.graphics.xmax - 1;
    YMAX = display_dev.graphics.ymax - 1;

    /* Set viewport for all the graphic output */
    set_viewport(0, margin.l , XMAX - margin.r, YMAX - margin.d, margin.u);
    return(0);

}

/*
 * Reset the display to text mode
 * 88/03/09 (BK) Hide cursor again.
 */
restore_graphics()
{
    initgraf (display_dev.text.mode, 0, display_dev.tclr[0]);
    hide_cursor();
}

show_graph(chart, flags)
int     chart, flags;
{
    int xvar, yvar;

    if (gdefs.plot != 5)
    {
        xvar = gdefs.graphs.type[chart][X];  /* The X variable */
        yvar = gdefs.graphs.type[chart][Y];  /* The Y variable */
```

```
    if (yvar == -1) return(1);

    /* Get the axis names */
    strcpy (vertical_axis, gdefs.graphs.name[chart][Y]);
    strcpy (horizontal_axis, gdefs.graphs.name[chart][X]);
    }

switch(gdefs.analysis)
    {
    case 1: switch(gdefs.plot)
        {
        case 1: return(ind_line_graph(yvar, chart, flags));
                break;
        case 2: return(ind_bar_graph(yvar, chart, flags));
                break;
        case 3: /* Y only*/
                return(ind_box_graph(yvar, chart, flags));
                break;
        case 4: /* X -vs- Y */
                if (xvar == -1) return(1);
                return(ind_scatter_graph(xvar, yvar, chart, flags));
                break;
        case 5: /* X -vs- Y */
                return(ind_nutrient_breakdown(chart, flags));
                break;

        }
        break;
    case 2: switch(gdefs.plot)
        {
        case 1: /* Y only*/
                return(ind_box_graph(yvar, chart, flags));
                break;
        case 2: /* X -vs- Y */
                if (xvar == -1) return(1);
                return(igp_scatter_graph(xvar, yvar, chart, flags));
                break;
        case 3:
                if (xvar == -1) return(1);
                return(igp_box_special(xvar, yvar, chart, flags));
                break;

        }
        break;
    case 3: switch(gdefs.plot)
        {
        case 1: return(sgp_bar_graph(yvar, chart, flags));
```

```c
                break;
        case 2: /* Y only*/
                return(sgp_box_graph(yvar, chart, flags));
                break;
        case 3: /* Y only*/
                return(sgp_box_special(yvar, chart, flags));
                break;
        }
        break;
    case 4: switch(gdefs.plot)
        {
        case 1: return(mgp_bar_graph(yvar, chart, flags));
                break;
        case 2: /* Y only*/
                return(mgp_box_special(yvar, chart, flags));
                break;
        }
        break;
    }

    return(0);

}

/* Input a new y range from the user */
/* 88/03/08 (BK)   Quit on <Esc>. */
/* 88/03/24 (BK)   No update unless valid line entered. */
get_user_y_range()
{
    char *s, buff[10];
    float low, high;
    int flag = 0, c;

    c = get_string(0, spacing.ch.v, "New Y axis (low,high) => ", buff, 9);
    if (c == ESC) return(flag);

    s = strscan(buff,',',0);
    if (s != NULL )
    {
        low = (float) atoi(s);
        if (low >= Min && low <= Max) { /* w[0].y.min = low; */ flag = 1; }
    }

    s = strscan(buff,',',1);
    if (s != NULL)
    {
        high = (float) atoi(s);
        if (high >= Min && high <= Max && high > low)
```

```c
        { /* w[0].y.max = high; */ flag += 2; }

    if (flag == 3) { w[0].y.min = low; w[0].y.max = high; }
    return(flag);
}

/* Input a new y range from the user */
/* 88/03/08 (BK)   Quit on <Esc>. */
/* 88/03/24 (BK)   No update unless valid line entered. */
get_user_x_range()
{
    char *s, buff[10];
    float low, high;
    int flag = 0, c;

    c = get_string(0, spacing.ch.v, "New X axis (low,high) => ", buff, 9);
    if (c == ESC) return(flag);

    s = strscan(buff,',',0);
    if (s != NULL)
    {
        low = (float) atoi(s);
        if (low >= Min && low <= Max )
            { /* w[0].x.min = low; */ flag = 1; }
    }

    s = strscan(buff,',',1);
    if (s != NULL)
    {
        high = (float) atoi(s);
        if (high >= Min && high <= Max && high > low)
            { /* w[0].x.max = high; */ flag += 2;}
    }

    if (flag == 3) { w[0].x.min = low; w[0].x.max = high; }
    return(flag);
}

/*
 *      Graphics cursor move
 */
g_write(c, row, col, lcol, color)
int c, row, col, lcol, color;
{
    fontch(0, c, lcol + (col * spacing.ch.h), row, color, 0);
}
```

```
graph_message(mess)
int mess;
{
    grrtulc(0, 0, XMAX, YMAX, gclr[0]);        /* Clear the screen */

    switch(mess)
    {
    case -1 : g_centers(0, "Can't plot fewer than three data points", YMAX/2,
                           0,XMAX, 0, gclr[1]);
              break;
    case  1 : g_centers(0, "Invalid graph (PgUp/PgDn for next graph)", YMAX/2,
                           0,XMAX, 0, gclr[1]);
              break;
    case  2 : g_centers(0, "Print (Y/N)? N", YMAX/2,
                           0,XMAX, 0, gclr[1]);
              break;
    case  3 : g_centers(0, "Enter a new range for Y", YMAX/2,
                           0,XMAX, 0, gclr[1]);
              break;
    case  4 : g_centers(0, "Enter a new range for X", YMAX/2,
                           0,XMAX, 0, gclr[1]);
              break;
    default: g_centers(0, "Unknown error", YMAX/2,
                           0,XMAX, 0, gclr[1]);
              break;
    }
}

graph_inquire(num)
int num;
{
    graph_message(num);
    return( (tolower(t_getkey()) == 'y') ? 1 : 0);
}

#define isstring(c)         (c > 31 && c < 127) ? 1 : 0

/* 88/03/21 (BK)   Added code to clear vertical gap below display area. */
/* 88/03/24 (BK)   Corrected backspace handling to clear vertical gap;
                   corrected <Home>, <End> keys. */
get_string(x, y, str, buff, limit)
```

```c
int x, y, limit;
char *str, *buff;
{
    int     row, col, len, pos;
    int     c, key, ret_val = 0;

    strnset(buff, '\0', limit+1);
    buff[0] = ' '; len = 1;
    /* Clear the display area */
    grrtulc(x, y-spacing.ch.v, XMAX, spacing.ch.v+spacing.ch.vgap, gclr[0]);

    /* Display the prompt */
    fhatsay (0, str, gclr[1], x, y);
    /* Retrieve the current cursor position */
    fcurget (&x, &y);

    col = x; row = y;
    pos = 0;
    while (ret_val == 0)
    {
        col = pos * (spacing.ch.h +spacing.ch.hgap) + x;
        row = y;
        gcurloc(col,row);   /* Position the cursor under the next character */

        /* Display the cursor and return the next key pressed */
        c = (gcurmove(1, &col, &row, &key) == 1) ? key : 0-key;
        switch (c)
        {
        case ESC :      ret_val = ESC;
                        break;

        case '\n':
        case '\r':      ret_val = CR;
                        break;

        case END :      pos = len-1;
                        break;

        case HOME:      pos = 0;
                        break;

        case C_LEFT:    if (pos > 0)
                            pos--;
                        break;

        case C_RIGHT:if (pos < len-1)
                            pos++;
                        break;

        case '\b' :     if (pos > 0)
                        {
                            if (pos == len-1)
```

```
                        { buff[pos] = '\0';
                          len--;
                        }
                      pos--;                /* Clear the display area */
                      col = pos * (spacing.ch.h +spacing.ch.hgap) + x;
                      grbxfill(col, y-spacing.ch.v,
                               col+spacing.ch.h, y+spacing.ch.vgap, gclr[0]);
                      buff[pos] = ' ';

        case '\t': c = ' ';
        default :  if (pos < limit && isstring(c))
                   {
                     if (pos == len-1)
                     {
                       len++;
                       buff[len] = '\0';
                     }
                     fontch (0, c, col, row, gclr[1], 0);
                     buff[pos] = (char) c;
                     pos++;
                   }
                   else
                     if (c < 0) ret_val = c;
                   else
                     continue;
                   break;
      }
    }
  /* Clear the display area. */
  grrtulc(x, y-spacing.ch.v, XMAX, spacing.ch.v+spacing.ch.vgap, gclr[0]);
  return (ret_val);
}

get_chart_size()
{
  int c, ret_val;

  ret_val = -1;
  grrtulc(0, 0, XMAX, YMAX, gclr[0]);               /* Clear the screen */
  g_centers(0, "Print Size (S/M/L)? S", YMAX/2, 0,XMAX, 0, gclr[1]);
  while (ret_val == -1)
  {
    c = tolower(t_getkey());
```

```
    switch(c)
    {
        case CR :
        case 's': ret_val = 0;
                  break;
        case 'm': ret_val = 1;
                  break;
        case 'l': ret_val = 2;
                  break;
        case ESC: ret_val = ESC;
                  break;
    }
}

return(ret_val);
}
```

FLOW.C

```
#include <stdio.h>
#include <ctype.h>
#include <dos.h>
#include <string.h>
#include <conio.h>
#include "..\struct.h"
#include "..\extern.h"

/*
 *      This function controls the overall flow from menu to menu
 *      using a finite automaton (DFA)
 *
 * 88/02/22 (BK)  Changed: ESC from verification screen quits
 *                properly to previous screen; ESC from plot
 *                selection screen does not clear flags.
 * 88/03/25 (BK)  Removed main screen command handling to avoid redisplay.
 */

flow_control()
{
   static int state=0;
   int        c;

   while (1)
   {
      switch (state)
      {
/*================= Main Menu =========================================*/
         case 0 :
            switch(menu_000())
            {
               /* Data Selection */
               case 3 :  state = 1;
                         break;
               /* Graph Selection */
               case 4 :  state = 6;
                         break;
               /* View Graph */
               case 5 :  view();
                         break;
               /* Exit Program */
               case 8 :  state = -1;
                         break;
```

```
                  }
                  break;

/*=============== Two way switch =================*/
     case 1 : if (get_flag(D_CHOSEN))        /* Were we here already */
                  state = 5;
              else
                  state = 2;
              break;

/*=============== Analysis Menu =================*/
     case 2 : reset_flags();                 /* Select Analysis */
              switch(menu_1())
                 {
              case 0  :
                  help_on (2, 5);
                  c = prompt(3,10,-1,"Define additional parameters (Y/N)?");
                  help_off ();            /* Yes */
                  if (c == 1)
                     {
                  set_flag (D_CHOSEN);
                  state = 3;
                     }
                  else
                  if (c == 0)             /* No */
                     {
                  set_flag (D_CHOSEN);
                  /* set_flag(P_DEFINED); */
                  state = 4;
                     }
                  break;
              case ESC: state = 0;
                  clear_all();
                  break;

                  }

              break;

/*=========== Define Parameters =================*/
     case 3 : switch(menu_2())
                 {
              case 0  :  state = 4;
                  set_flag(P_DEFINED);
                  break;
              case ESC: if (escape(1)) state = 2;
                  break;
                  }
```

```
            break;

/*================= Verification Screen ==================*/
/* Initial entry. ESC quits to previous menu, either analysis or
 * parameters. F10 exits to main menu.
 */
    case 4 : switch(menu_3())
             {
             case 0 :  state = 0;   /* Main Menu */
                       break;
             case ESC: if (escape(2))
                       { if (get_flag(P_DEFINED)) state = 3;
                         else state = 2;
                       }
                       break;
             }
             break;

/*================= Verification Screen ==================*/
    case 5 :  menu_3();
              state = 0;
              break;

/*================= Select Plot to View ==================*/
/* ESC quits without changing flags. F10 exits to select variables.
 */
    case 6 :/* clear_flag(G_VARIABLES); */
             switch(menu_004())
             {
             case  0 :  state = 7;
                        set_flag(G_SELECTED);
                        break;
             case ESC :  state = 0;
                        /* clear_flag(G_SELECTED); */
                        break;
             }
             break;

/*================= Select Variables ==================*/
    case 7 : if (get_flag(G_VARIABLES))
                state = 0;
             else
                state = 8;
             break;
```

```
/*===================  Analysis Screen   ====================*/
   case 8 : switch(menu_005())
            {
            case -1:    state = 0;
                        clear_flag(G_SELECTED);
                        break;
            case 0 :    state = 0;
                        set_flag(G_VARIABLES);
                        break;
            case ESC:   state = 6;
                        clear_flag(G_VARIABLES | G_SELECTED);
                        break;
            }
            break;

/*===================  Exit the program   ====================*/
   case -1: return (0);
   }
} /*  flow_control() */

/*
 * Evaluate the parameter definiton situation and recommend a new state
 */
escape(where)
int where;
{
   int i;

   i = 1;

   switch(where)
   {
   case 1 : /* From parameter definition screen */
            if (get_flag(P_DEFINED))
            {
            message(1, "All changes will be lost");
            if ( prompt (0, 2, -1, "Proceed (Y/N)?") )
                clear_parameters();
            else
                i = 0;
            message(-1, "");
            }
            break;
   case 2 : /* From data verification screen */
```

```
           if (records_exist())
           {
               message(1, "All changes will be lost");
               if ( prompt (0, 2, -1, "Proceed (Y/N)?") )
                   clear_data_sets();
               else
                   i = 0;
               message(-1, "");
           }
           break;
       }
       return(i);
   }
```

IGP.C (partial listing)

```c
#include <stdio.h>
#include <stdlib.h>
#include <search.h>
#include "..\struct.h"
#include "..\extern.h"
#include "..\dinescor.h"
#include "..\graph.h"

extern float Spearman();
extern float Kruskal_Wallis();

/*               This file contains the code for plotting a single
 *    igp.c  -              group analysis
 */

/*-------------------------igp_box_special---------------------------*
 * Plots box & whiskers of delta Y by category.
 *
 * 88/02/10 (BK)   Revised to calculate Kruskal-Wallis one-way
 *                 analysis of variance.
 * 88/02/23 (BK)   Added return(-1) if each category has < 3 points.
 * 88/02/29 (BK)   Included n[i] in printed output.
 * 88/03/08 (BK)   Changed to allow x range to be modified.
 * 88/03/17 (BK)   Added test statistic display.
 *-------------------------------------------------------------------*/

igp_box_special(x, y, plot, flags)
int x, y, plot, flags;
{
    float high[5], low[5], median[5], lower[5], upper[5];
    int   k, i, c, n[5], x1, y1, x2, y2, p, categories, empty;
    float x1, xh, y1, yh, max_val, min_val, width, space;
    float Dj[5][50];
    char outstr[BUFSIZ];

    categories = ncategories(x);
    if (categories == 0)
        return(-1);
    p = get_param(x);

    load_array (Y,  0, 0, y);
    load_array (X , 0, 0, x);
    /* Do not use missing values */
    remove_unknown_data (Y, 2);
```

```c
empty = 1;
for (i = 0; i < 5; i++) n[i] = 0;
for(i=0; i < categories; i++)
{

    /* Load the array with all values from one category */
    load_category (i+1);
    n[i] = npoints[RHY];

    /* Generate the data for the analysis. */
    if (flags & 8)
    for (k = 0; k < n[i]; k++) Dj[i][k] = dvalue[RHY][k];

    if (n[i] < 3) continue; else empty = 0;
    sort_array(RHY);        /* Sort the array in increasing order */
    calculate_box_n_whiskers(RHY, &high[i], &(low[i]), &median[i],
                             &lower[i], &upper[i]);
}

if (empty) return(-1);

max_val = 0.0; min_val = 0.0;
for(i=0; i < categories; i++)
{
    if (n[i] < 3) continue;
    max_val = (float) max( high[i], max_val);
    min_val = (float) min( low[i] , min_val);
}

w[0].y.min = 0.0; w[0].y.max = 10.0;   /* Set the height of the window */
if (flags & 2) { w[0].x.min = min_val; w[0].x.max = max_val; }

/* Clear the screen and display the title */
display_title("%s by %s Group",vertical_axis,
              ((p == -1) ? "SEX" : params[p].pname));

x_axis( plot, Y, 3, flags);
use_plotting_limits();

width = 0.5; space = 1.5; yl = 0.75;
/* Draw the box */
for(i=0; i < categories; i++)
{
    yh = yl + width;
    if (n[i] >= 3)
    {
```

```
      if (p != -1)
         plot_box_n_whiskers(yl, yh, high[i], low[i], median[i], lower[i],
                             upper[i], params[p].cname[i], gclr[3]);

      else
         plot_box_n_whiskers(yl, yh, high[i], low[i], median[i], lower[i],
                             upper[i], ((i==0) ? "MALES" : "FEMALES"), gclr[3]);

      }
      yl = yh + space;

   if (flags & 8)
   {  sprintf(outstr, "K-W: H = %.2f, N = %d", Kruskal_Wallis(Dj, n), n[0]);
      for (i = 1; i < categories; i++) sprintf(outstr+strlen(outstr), ",%d", n[i]);
      display_message(outstr);
   }
   if (flags & 4) print_graph();
   return (2 | 4 | 8 | 32);  /* X, print, statistic, grid */
}

load_category (category)
int category;
{
   int i, cnt;

   npoints[RHY] = 0;            /* Clear the array */
   for (cnt = i = 0; i < npoints[X]; i++)
   {
      if (category == (int)dvalue[X][i])
      {
         dvalue[RHY][cnt] = dvalue[Y][i];
         dptr[RHY][cnt]  = &(dvalue[RHY][cnt]);
         npoints[RHY] = ++cnt;
      }
   }
}
```

INDIVID.C (partial listing)

```c
#include <stdio.h>
#include <stdlib.h>
#include <search.h>
#include "..\struct.h"
#include "..\extern.h"
#include "..\dinescor.h"
#include "..\graph.h"

y_axis(plot, grid)
int plot, grid;
{ int y1, y2;

    y1 = rnd(w[0].y.min); y2 = rnd(w[0].y.max);
    plot_y_axis (&y1, &y2, gdefs.graphs.unit[plot][Y], grid & 32);
    w[0].y.min = (float) y1; w[0].y.max = (float) y2;
}

/* 88/02/12  (BK)    Added unit as argument to plot_x_axis2.
 * 88/02/19  (BK)    Removed case 2 (plot_x_axis1).
 * 88/03/08  (BK)    Changed case 5 from special to axis3; removed case 4. */

x_axis(plot, var, type, grid)
int var, plot, type, grid;
{ int  x1, x2;

    x1 = rnd(w[0].x.min);  x2 = rnd(w[0].x.max);

    if (type == 1 || type == 3 || type == 5)
        plot_x_axis3( &x1, &x2, gdefs.graphs.unit[plot][var], grid & 32);

    w[0].x.min = (float) x1;  w[0].x.max = (float) x2;
}
```

IO.C (partial listing)

```c
#include <stdlib.h>
#include <stdio.h>
#include <ctype.h>
#include <dos.h>
#include <string.h>
#include <conio.h>
#include <malloc.h>
#include "..\struct.h"
#include "..\extern.h"
#include "..\dinescor.h"

clear_dine_arrays(rec)
RECORD *rec;
{
    int i;

    for(i=0;i<FPM; i++)
        {
        rec->actual[i]  = 0.0;
        rec->high[i]    = Unknown;
        rec->low[i]     = Unknown;
        }

    for(i=FPM;i<FPM+MaxParams; i++)
        {
        rec->actual[i]  = Unknown;
        rec->high[i]    = Unknown;
        rec->low[i]     = Unknown;
        }

    rec->actual[WEIGHT]  = Unknown;
    rec->high[WEIGHT]    = Unknown;
    rec->low[WEIGHT]     = Unknown;
}
```

LOAD.C

```c
#include <stdio.h>
#include <stdlib.h>
#include <search.h>
#include <string.h>
#include <varargs.h>
#include "..\struct.h"
#include "..\extern.h"
#include "..\dinescor.h"
#include "..\graph.h"

load_array(array, group, screen, var)
int array, group, screen, var;
{

RECORD *ptr;
int    variable, point = 0;

/* Only deal with single user and group for now */
ptr = vscreens[group][screen];
while (ptr != NULL)
    {
    if (var == -1)
        dvalue[array][point] = (float) point;
    else
        {
        switch(array)
            {
            case  X:
            case  Y:  dvalue[array][point] = ptr->actual[var];
                      break;

            case RLY:
            case RLX:  dvalue[array][point] = ptr->low[var];
                       break;

            case RHY:
            case RHX:  dvalue[array][point] = ptr->high[var];
                       break;
            }

        dptr[array][point]    = &(dvalue[array][point]);
        point++;
        ptr = ptr->next;
```

```
        }
    npoints[array] = point;
}

remove_unknown_data(var, flag)
int var, flag;
{
    int c, i;

    c = 0;
    switch(flag)
    {
    case 0 : i = npoints[var];
             while (c < i)
             {
                 if (dvalue[var][c] == Unknown)
                 {
                     delete_element (var, c);
                     i--;
                 }
                 else
                     c++;
             }
             break;
    case 1 : i = npoints[var];
             while (c < i)
             {
                 if (dvalue[var][c] == Unknown)
                 {
                     delete_element (X, c);
                     delete_element (Y, c);
                     delete_element (RHY, c);
                     delete_element (RLY, c);
                     delete_element (RHX, c);
                     delete_element (RLX, c);
                     i--;
                 }
                 else
                     c++;
             }
             break;
    case 2 : i = npoints[var];
             while (c < i)
             {
                 if (dvalue[X][c] == Unknown || dvalue[Y][c] == Unknown)
                 {
```

```
                delete_element (X, c);
                delete_element (Y, c);
                i--;
            }
            else
                c++;
        }
        break;
case 3 : i = npoints[var];
        while (c < i)
        {
            if (dvalue[X][c] == Unknown || dvalue[Y][c] == Unknown)
            {
                delete_element (X, c);
                delete_element (Y, c);
                delete_element (RHY, c);
                delete_element (RLY, c);
                delete_element (RHX, c);
                delete_element (RLX, c);
                i--;
            }
            else
                c++;
        }
        break;
    }
}

/* Remove the element from the array and slide the rest down one */
delete_element (array, element)
int array, element;
{
    while (element < (npoints[array] - 1) )
    {
        dvalue[array][element] = dvalue[array][element+1];
        element++;
    }
    if (npoints[array] > 0) npoints[array]--;
}

int compare(arg1, arg2)
float **arg1, **arg2;
{
    if ( **arg1 < **arg2)
```

```
        return(-1);
    else
        if (**arg1 > **arg2)
            return(1);
        else
            return(0);
}

sort_arrays()
{ int i;

    for (i = 0; i < 6; i++)
    {
        if (npoints[i] > 0)
            qsort((void *) &(dptr[i][0]), (size_t) npoints[i], sizeof (float *), compare);
    }

}

sort_array(array)
int array;
{

    if (npoints[array] > 0)
        qsort((void *) &(dptr[array][0]), (size_t) npoints[array], sizeof (float *), compare);
}
```

MAIN.C

```c
#include <stdio.h>
#include <stdlib.h>
#include <ctype.h>
#include <dos.h>
#include <string.h>
#include <conio.h>
#include <varargs.h>

#include "struct.h"
#include "extern.h"

char    clr[TColors];            /* Text Color Table */
char    gclr[GColors];           /* Graphics Color Table */

int     message_row[3] = { 24, 23, 1};
int     message_color[3];

DISPLAY_DEV    display_dev;

/*     Declare all global variables */

struct  gdefs gdefs;             /* Define all the
global flags */
struct Params Params[MaxParams];    /* Parameter names
and types */
SCREENS *vscreens[MaxGroups][2];

ERROR   device_info;

/* 88/03/04 (BK) Removed compatibility handling. */

main(argc, argv)
int argc; char *argv[];
{
    int i;

/*    if (argc == 2)
    {
        switch(atoi(argv[1]))
        {
```

```
            case 0 : b_compatibality(1, COLOR);
                     break;
            case 1 : b_compatibality(1, MONO);
                     break;

        }

    }

*/

    b_scrollup(0, 0, 24, 79, 0, wattr(White, Black));
    cr_error_install(&device_info);
    hide_cursor();
    logo(0);
    if ( init_globals() != -1)
    { extern int help();
      set_menu_scroll_bar (clr[5]);
      t_set_key (F_1);              /* Set help activation key */
      t_set_function (help);         /* Set the function pointer */
      t_flushkey();
      flow_control();
      release_screen(0);
      release_screen(1);
      b_scrollup(0, 0, 24, 79, 0, wattr(White, Black));
      chdir(gdefs.path[0]);

    }

    show_cursor();

}


/*
 * Open the warning box and output the message in the window
 * if a paramter list is included pass it to the w_printc function
 * which will use the paramater list as arguments
 *
 * 88/03/23 (BK)   Recoded and restored multiple-line output.
 */
void
warning(va_alist)
va_dcl
{
    WINDOW   *warning_window;
    char     buff[BUFSIZ];
    char     line[2][41];
    char     *mess, *ptr, *result;
    va_list  arg_ptr;
```

```
    int lineno, m,c, vpage, row, col;
    int bp, i;

    va_start(arg_ptr);
    mess = va_arg (arg_ptr, char *);
    vsprintf (buff, mess, arg_ptr);
    va_end  (arg_ptr);

/*    if (strlen(buff) > 39) return; */

/* If buffer is longer than 39 characters, determine breakpoint (space
 * nearest and not after 39th character, or 39th if no space), and split.
 */

    if (strlen(buff) > 39)
    { bp = 39; for (i = 0; i < 38; i++) if (buff[i] == ' ') bp = i+1;
      strncpy (line[0], buff, bp);
      strncpy (line[1], &buff[bp], (int) min (strlen (buff)-bp, 39));
      line[0][bp] = line[1][(int) min (strlen (buff)-bp, 39)] = '\0';
    }
    else
    { strcpy (line[0], buff);
      strcpy (line[1], "");
    }

    b_video_mode(&m ,&c, &vpage);

    b_readpos (&row, &col, vpage);
/* Print out the two lines */
    warning_window = wopen (9, 20, 13, 59, clr[2], Border);
    b_centers(line[0], 10, 21, 58, clr[2], vpage);
    b_centers(line[1], 11, 21, 58, clr[2], vpage);
    b_centers("Press any key to continue", 12, 21, 58, clr[2], vpage);

/* Wait */
    t_flushkey();
    t_getkey();
    wclose(warning_window);
    b_move (row, col, vpage);
}

/* 88/02/18 (BK)   Added input type 4: long int. */

prompt(input_type, ur, uc, mess, va_alist)
    int   input_type, ur, uc;
    char  *mess;
```

```
va_dcl
{
    char     *response;
    va_list   arg_ptr;
    int       key, len, col, size;
    char      *str;
    WINDOW    *win;
    int       lr, lc, auto_scale;
    int       ret_val;

    /* If upper column =
       -1 : Center          [ Character Box ]
       -2 : Left Justify
       -3 : Right Justify
    */
    if (uc < 0)
    {
        auto_scale = uc;
        uc = 0;
    }
    else
        auto_scale = 0;

    ret_val = -1;
    len = strlen(mess);

    /* Truncate the string */
    if (len > (78 - uc))
    {
        mess[78-uc] = '\0';
        len = 78-uc;
    }

    if (input_type == 1 || input_type == 4)
    {
        va_start(arg_ptr);
        response = va_arg (arg_ptr, char *);
        size = va_arg (arg_ptr, int);
        va_end (arg_ptr);
        if (size > len) len = size;
    }

    lr = ur + 3;
    lc = uc + ( (len < 30) ? 30 : len) + 2;

    /* If upper column = -1 center the box in the x direction */
```

```
if (auto_scale)
{
    switch(auto_scale)
    {
        case -1 : /* Center */
            uc = (78 - lc) / 2;
            lc += uc;
            break;
        case -3 : /* Right Justify */
            uc = 78 - lc;
            lc = 79;
            break;
    }
}
/*    Open a window */
win = wopen(ur, uc, lr, lc, clr[3], Border);
save_cursor();
hide_cursor();
/* Center the message in the window */
b_centers(mess, ur+1, uc+1, lc, clr[3], 0);
t_flushkey();
switch (input_type)
{
    case 0 :    /* Input a Y/N/ESC output 1/0/0 */
        while (ret_val == -1)
        {
            key = t_getkey();
            if ( key > 0 )
            {
                if ( key == 'Y' || key == 'y')
                    ret_val = 1;
                else
                    if ( key == 'N' || key == 'n' || key == ESC)
                        ret_val = 0;
            }
        }
        break;
    case 1 :    /* Input a string */
        col = (lc - uc - size)/2 + 1;
        show_cursor();
        ret_val = wgets(response, ur+2, uc+col, size, clr[0]);
        break;
    case 2 :    /* Any Character */
        while (ret_val == -1)
        {
```

```
                    key = t_getkey();
                    if ( key > 0 && (isalnum(key) || key == ESC) )
                        ret_val = key;
                }
                break;
        case 3 :
                /* Input a Y/N/ESC   return 0, 1, ESC */
                while (ret_val == -1)
                {
                    key = t_getkey();
                    if ( key > 0 )
                    {
                        if ( key == 'Y' || key == 'y')
                            ret_val = 1;
                        else
                            if ( key == 'N' || key == 'n' || key == ESC)
                                ret_val = (key == ESC) ? ESC : 0;
                    }
                }
                break;
        case 4 :
                /* Input an integer */
                col = (lc - uc - size)/2 + 1;
                show_cursor();
                ret_val = wgetl((long *) response, ur+2, uc+col, size, clr[0]);
    }
    restore cursor();
    wclose(win);
    return(ret_val);
}


clear_screen(attr)
char attr;
{
    b_scrollup (2, 0, 22, 79, 0, attr);

}

/*
 * Open the warning box and output the message in the window
 * if a paramter list is included pass it to the w_printc function
 * which will use the paramater list as arguments
 */

void
message(option, va_alist)
int option;
```

```c
va_dcl
{
	va_list	arg_ptr;
	char	*mess, buff[81];
	char	attr=0;
	int	row = 1;

	row = abs(option);
	b_scrollup (row, 0, row, 79, 0, clr[4]);

	va_start(arg_ptr);
	mess = va_arg (arg_ptr, char *);

	if (mess != NULL)
	{
		vsprintf (buff, mess, arg_ptr);
		va_end (arg_ptr);

		if (option > 0)
			attr = clr[4] | Blink;
		else
			attr = clr[4];

		b_centers (buff, row, 0, 79, attr, 0);
	}
}

int
set_flag(flag)
int flag;
{
	gdefs.flags |= flag;
	return(gdefs.flags);
}

int
clear_flag(flag)
int flag;
{
	gdefs.flags &= ~flag;
	return(gdefs.flags);
}

int
get_flag(f)
{
```

```c
	return( ((gdefs.flags & f) == f) ? 1 : 0);
}

int
reset_flags(void)
{
	int old_flags;

	old_flags = gdefs.flags;
	gdefs.flags = 0;
	return(old_flags);
}

restore_session()
{
	int ok, brk, i;

	ok = 1; brk = 0;

	/* If data was modifyed (either restored and changed or newly entered)*/
	if (get_flag(D_MODIFY | D_EXIST | D_CHOSEN))
	{
		while (!brk)
		{
			message(1,"All data and parameters will be lost");
			help_on (0, 8);
			i = prompt(3,10,-1,"Save now  (Y/N)?");
			help_off();
			message(-1,"");
			switch (i)
			{
				case ESC : ok = 0;
					   brk = 1;
					   break;
				case  0  : brk = 1;
					   break;
				case  1  :if (save_to_file() != 0)
					    brk = 1;
					   break;
			}
		}
	}
	return (ok);
}
```

```c
clear_data()
{
int i;
help_on(0, 2);
i = prompt(0,10,-1,"Clear all data and additional parameters  (Y/N)?");
help_off();
if (i) clear_all();
return (i);
}

clear_all()
{
    release_screen(0);
    release_screen(1);
    clear_parameters();
    reset_flags();
    gdefs.analysis = 0;
    gdefs.gcnt = 0;
    gdefs.three_day = 0;
    gdefs.plot = 0;
}

clear_data_sets()
{
    release_screen(0);
    release_screen(1);
    clear_flag (D_EXIST | D_MODIFY | G_SELECTED | G_VARIABLES);
}

/* Cursor hiding, saving, restoring functions */
#define STACK_SIZE    10
static  int cursor_state;
static  int cursor_stack[STACK_SIZE+1] = { 0, };

/* Push the cursor state onto the cursor stack */

int
save_cursor(void)
{
    int tos;                   /* Top of stack */
```

```c
    tos = cursor_stack[0];
    if (tos == STACK_SIZE)       /* Stack Overflow */
        return(-1);
    else
    {
        tos++;
        cursor_stack[0] = tos;
        cursor_stack[tos] = cursor_state;
        return(cursor_state);
    }
}

/* Pop the cursor state from the cursor stack */

int
restore_cursor(void)
{
    int tos;                     /* Top of stack */

    tos = cursor_stack[0];
    if (tos == 0)                /* Stack Underflow */
        return(-1);
    else
    {
        cursor_state = cursor_stack[tos];
        tos--;                   /* Pop */
        cursor_stack[0] = tos;
        if (cursor_state == 0)
            hide_cursor();
        else
            show_cursor();
        return(cursor_state);
    }
}

void
show_cursor(void)
{
    b_cursor (7,7,0);
    cursor_state = 1;
}

void
```

```
hide_cursor(void)
{
  b_cursor (7,7,1);
  cursor_state = 0;
}
```

MENU_000.C

```c
#include <stdio.h>
#include <ctype.h>
#include <conio.h>
#include "..\struct.h"
#include "..\extern.h"

static MENU  main_menu[] = {
"Main Menu"                     ,  0,
""                              , -2,
"Path Selection          [P]"   ,  1,
"Restore Session         [R]"   ,  2,
""                              , -2,
"Data Selection          [D]"   ,  3,
"Graph Selection         [G]"   ,  4,
"View Graph              [V]"   ,  5,
"Export Data             [E]"   ,  6,
""                              , -2,
"Save Session            [S]"   ,  7,
"Exit Program            [X]"   ,  8,
""                              , -2,
"Clear Data              [C]"   ,  9,
"", -2,
"Select with arrow keys", 0 ,
"or press letter", 0 ,
};

static MENU_KEYS  menu_keys[] = {
        { F_1,  0 },    /* HELP */
        { F_10, 8 },    /* DONE */
        { ESC,  8 },    /* EXIT */
        { F_9,  1 },    /* Path Selection */
        { 'P',  1 },
        { 'R',  2 },
        { F_5,  2 },
        { 'D',  3 },
        { 'G',  4 },
        { 'V',  5 },
        { 'E',  6 },
        { 'S',  7 },
        { 'X',  8 },
        { 'C',  9 },
};
```

```
/*
 *
 */
/* 88/03/25 (BK)    Top Level Menu (Main Menu)

                    Internalized command handling to avoid redisplay;
                    return values are 3 (data selection); 4 (graph
                    selection); 5 (view graph); 8 (exit). */

menu_000()
{
    static int   keypressed;        /*      User key pressed */
    int          selection;         /*      Menu Selection   */
    int          ret_val;
    int          c;

    ret_val = 0;
    status(-1); directions(0);  pfkeys(7);
    logo(0);
    cls();

    while (ret_val == 0)
    {
        set_menu_keys (menu_keys, dim(menu_keys) );
        selection = get_menu_selection(&keypressed, main_menu, dim(main_menu),
                                        -1, -1, clr[0], Border);

        message(-1,"");
        switch (selection)
        {

/* Help */    case 0  : help (1,0);
/* Selection */           break;

/* Path */    case 1  : change_directory ();
/* Selection */           break;

/* Restore */ case 2  : call restore_session ();
/* Session */             break;

/* Data */    case 3  : ret_val = 3;
/* Selection */           break;

/* Graph */   case 4  : if (get_flag (D_EXIST | D_CHOSEN)) ret_val = 4;
/* Selection */           else warning ("Please use data selection first");
                          break;
```

```
/* View */    case 5   : if (get_flag (G_SELECTED | D_EXIST)) ret_val = 5;
/* Graph */                 else warning ("Please use graph selection first");
                            break;

/* Export */  case 6   : call export_data ();
/* Data */                  break;

/* Save */    case 7   : call save_session ();
/* Session */               break;

/* Exit */    case 8   : if (exit_program ()) ret_val = 8;
/* Program */               break;

/* Clear */   case 9   : clear_data ();
/* Data */                  break;

        }

        return (ret_val);

}

call_restore_session ()
{ if (restore_session ()) load_from_file ();
}

call_export_data ()
{ if (records_exist ()) output_data ();
  else warning ("No data to export");
}

call_save_session ()
{ if (get_flag (D_CHOSEN)) save_to_file ();
  else warning ("Nothing to be saved");
}

/*---------------------------exit_program---------------------------*
 * Prompts to confirm; if data modified, prompts to save session.
 * <Esc> backs up one step. Returns 1 to exit, 0 not to exit.
 *------------------------------------------------------------------*/

exit_program ()
{ int c;

  while (1)
  { help_on (0, 3);
    c = prompt (0, 10, -1, "Exit program (Y/N) ?");
```

```
help_off ();
if (c == 0) return (0);                              /* No, <Esc> */
else                                                 /* Yes */
    if (get_flag (D_MODIFY))                         /* modified */
    { while (1)
        { help_on (0, 7);
          c = prompt (3, 10, -1, "Save session (Y/N)?");
          help_off ();
          if (c == 0) return (1);                    /* No */
          else if (c == 1)                           /* Yes */
          { if (save_to_file ()) return (1);         /* successful */
              else continue; }                       /* unsuccessful */
            else break; } }                          /* <Esc> */
      else return (1); }                             /* not modified */

}
```

MENU_001.C

```c
#include <stdio.h>
#include <conio.h>
#include <string.h>
#include "..\struct.h"
#include "..\extern.h"

static MENU menu[] = {
        "Analysis Type Menu", 0 ,
        "", -2,
        "Individual                 [1]", 1,
        "Single Group               [2]", 2,
        "Single Group (Before/After) [3]", 3,
        "Multiple Group (Before/After) [4]", 4,
        "", -2,
        "Select with arrow keys", 0 ,
        "or press number", 0 ,
        };

static MENU_KEYS menu_keys[] = {
                { F 1, 0},
                { ESC, ESC},
                { '1', 1},
                { '2', 2},
                { '3', 3},
                { '4', 4},
                };

/*
 *              Type of analysis
 */

menu_1()
{
    int    selection, keypressed=0, ret_val = -1, c;

    status(-1); directions(0); pfkeys(0);
    cls();

    while (ret_val == -1)
        {
        /* Get the type of analysis */
        set_menu_keys(menu_keys, dim(menu_keys));
        selection = get_menu_selection(&keypressed, menu, dim(menu),
```

```
                                                        -1, -1, clr[0], Border);
    switch (selection)
        {
        case 0  : help(2,0);
                  break;
        case ESC : ret_val = ESC;
                   gdefs.analysis = 0;
                   break;
        default : gdefs.analysis = selection;
                  help_on (2, 1);
                  c = prompt(3, 3, -1, "Use three-day analysis (Y/N)?");
                  help_off();
                  if (c != ESC)
                      {
                      gdefs.three_day = c;
                      if ( get_group_name() == CR)
                          ret_val = CR;
                      }
                  break;
        }

    if (ret_val == CR)
        return(0);
    else
        return(ESC);
    }

/*
 * Get the name of the individual or groups, etc
 * 88/02/29 (BK)   Changed to allow ESC from number of groups.
 */
get_group_name()
    {
    char buff[Gsize+1];
    char lbuff[30];
    int key, i;
    long gcnt;

    strcpy(buff,"");
    gdefs.gcnt = 1;
    switch(gdefs.analysis)
        {
        case 1 : /* Individual Analysis */
                 default_keys();
```

```
            help_on (2, 2);
            key = prompt (1, 2, -1, "Individual's name:", buff, Gsize);
            help_off();
            if (key == CR)
                {
                strrmtb(buff);
                if (gdefs.group_name[0]  != NULL)
                    free(gdefs.group_name[0]);
                gdefs.group_name[0] = strdup(buff);
                }
            break;
    case 2 :  /* Single Group */
    case 3 :
            default_keys();
            help_on (2, 3);
            key = prompt (1, 2, -1, "Group's name:", buff, Gsize);
            help_off();
            if (key == CR)
                {
                strrmtb(buff);
                if (gdefs.group_name[0]  != NULL)
                    free(gdefs.group_name[0]);
                gdefs.group_name[0] = strdup(buff);
                }
            break;

    case 4 :  /* Multiple Groups */
            gcnt = 0L;
            while ((gcnt <= 0L || gcnt > (long) MaxGroups) && key != ESC)
                {
                default_keys();
                help_on (2, 4);
                key = prompt (4, 2, -1, "Number of groups:", &gcnt, 1);
                help_off();
                if (key == CR)
                    {
                    if (gcnt > 0L && gcnt <= (long) MaxGroups)
                        key = input_group_names((int) gcnt);
                    }
                }
            break;
    }
    return (key);
}
```

```
input_group_names(gcnt)
int gcnt;
{
    char buff[Gsize+1];
    char lbuff[30];
    int key, i;

    for (i=0; i < gcnt; i++)
    {
        strcpy(buff,"");
        sprintf(lbuff, "Group %d's name:",i+1);
        default_keys();
        help_on (2, 3);
        key = prompt(1, 2, -1, lbuff, buff, Gsize);
        help_off();
        switch(key)
        {
            case CR : strrmtb(buff);
                if (strcmp(buff,"") == 0)
                    sprintf(buff,"Group %d",i+1);

                if (gdefs.group_name[i] != NULL)
                    free(gdefs.group_name[i]);

                gdefs.group_name[i] = strdup(buff);
                break;

            case ESC: gdefs.gcnt = 0;
                return(ESC);
                break;

        } /* Switch */

    }/* For loop */
    gdefs.gcnt = gcnt;
    return(CR);
}
```

MENU_002.C (partial listing)

```c
#include <stdio.h>
#include <ctype.h>
#include <dos.h>
#include <string.h>
#include <conio.h>
#include <stdlib.h>
#include "..\struct.h"
#include "..\extern.h"

#define BASE_ROW    4    /* Base row for first parameter record */
#define BASE_COL    1    /* Base col for first parameter record */
#define HEIGHT      2    /* Distance in row between records */
#define HEADER      3
#define MaxFields   6
#define maxfields(rec) ((ptemp[rec].ptype == 1) ? 1 : ptemp[rec].ptype+1)

#define ROW    0
#define COL    1

/* Relative column locations for fields */
static int    column[7] = {    2,    /* Parameter Name Field */
                              15,    /* Units or First Category */
                              28,    /* Second Category */
                              41,    /* Third Category */
                              54,    /* Fourth Category */
                              67,    /* Fifth Category */
                           };

/* Relative widths for columns */
static int    width[7] = { 10, 10, 10, 10, 10, 10 };

static struct  Params  ptemp[MaxParams];  /* Temporary parameter structure */

static char    *undefined = "██████████";

static int pcnt;    /* parameter count 1..5 */
static int rec, field;

/* 88/02/17 (BK)  Removed call to verify_data.
*/
menu_2 ()
{
```

```c
int  c, not_ok;
int  paratype;
char buff[12];
int  i,selection, input=1;
int  ret_val;
int  param, lastparam;
int  old pcnt;
struct Params *p;

pcnt = 0;
cls();
put_up_grid();               /* Display the parameter definition grid */

/* Transfer the current parameter definitions into a temporary structure*/
for(i=0;i<MaxParams;i++)
{
    memcpy ((void *) &ptemp[i], (void *) &params[i], sizeof(struct Params));
    if (ptemp[i].ptype > 0) pcnt++;
    draw_param_rec( (struct Params *) &ptemp[i], i );
}

status(-1); pfkeys(1); directions(2);
ret_val = 0;
field = rec = 0;
while (ret_val == 0)
{
    highlight (clr[5]);             /* Highlight the field */
    help_on (3, 0);
    c = t_getkey();
    help_off ();
    highlight (clr[0]);            /* remove the highlight*/
    switch (c)
    {
        case C_UP:    update (ROW, -1);
                      break;
        case C_DOWN:  update (ROW, 1);
                      break;
        case C_LEFT:  update (COL, -1);
                      break;
        case C_RIGHT: update (COL, 1);
                      break;
        case ESC :    if (parameters_changed())
                      {
                          message(1, "All changes will be lost");
                          if ( prompt (0, 2, -1, "Proceed (Y/N)?") )
                              ret_val = ESC;
```

```c
                message(-1, "");
            }
            else
                ret_val = ESC;
            break;     /*    Done    */
    case F_10:
            ret_val = 1;
            break;
    case CR :
            modify();
            break;
    default :
            if (c > 0 && isalnum(c))
            {
                t_ungetkey(c);
                modify();
            }
            break;
        }
    }

    if (ret_val != ESC)
    {
        /* Save the new parameter definitions */
        for(i=0; i<MaxParams; i++)
        {
            p = &ptemp[i];
            memcpy ((void *) &params[i], (void *) p, sizeof(struct Params));
        }
        gdefs.pcnt = pcnt;
        return (0);
    }
    else
        return(ESC);
}
```

```
MENU_003.C

#include <stdlib.h>
#include <stdio.h>
#include <ctype.h>
#include <dos.h>
#include <string.h>
#include <conio.h>
#include <malloc.h>
#include "..\struct.h"
#include "..\extern.h"
#include "..\dinescor.h"

#define FC          1           /* First screen column */
#define FR          7           /* First screen row */
#define LR          20          /* Last screen row */
#define Max_Record  LR-FR+1

/*      Location in row, col for each region */
static  int  locx_y[11][2] = {

        { FR,   FC + 2 },       /* Date of analysis */
        { FR,   FC + 11 },      /* Number of days in file */
        { FR,   FC + 19 },      /* Weight */
        { FR,   FC + 23 },      /* Data filename */
        { FR,   FC + 36 },      /* Day to use in analysis */
        { FR,   FC + 45 },      /* Parameter window # 1 */
        { FR,   FC + 56 },      /* Parameter window # 2 */
        { FR,   FC + 67 },      /* Parameter window # 3 */
        { FR-3, FC + 45 },      /* Parameter title # 1 */
        { FR-3, FC + 56 },      /* Parameter title # 2 */
        { FR-3, FC + 67 },      /* Parameter title # 3 */

        };

/*      Size in number of rows, number of columns for each region */
static  int  sizex_y[11][2] = {

        {16,  8 },      /* Date of analysis */
        {16,  7 },      /* Number of days in file */
        {16,  3 },      /* Weight */
        {16, 12 },      /* Data filename */
        {16,  8 },      /* Day to use in analysis */
        {16, 10 },      /* Parameter window # 1 */
        {16, 10 },      /* Parameter window # 2 */
        {16, 10 },      /* Parameter window # 3 */
```

```
static
char    *line_message[4] = {
                        { 1, 10}, /* Parameter title # 1 */
                        { 1, 10}, /* Parameter title # 2 */
                        { 1, 10}, /* Parameter title # 3 */
                        "Individual Analysis",
                        "Single Group Analysis",
                        "Single Group Analysis",
                        "Multiple Group Analysis",
                };

/* get the screen row for a logical record */
#define get_row(rec)            FR + rec - u_record

#define Visible_Records         Max_Record

static int      vertical_bars[9] = { 1, 10, 18, 22, 35, 44, 55, 66 , 77};
static char     signature[5] = { '-', 'C', 'R', '\n', '\0' };
static int      fields[4] = { 1, -1, -1, -1 };
static int      locate[3] = { FC + 45, FC + 56, FC + 67 };
static int      field, record, window, group;
static int      u_record, l_record, tot_records;
static int      current_scr = 0;

static int      cursor_movement = 0;            /* Column move */

set_cursor_movement(n)
int n;
{
        cursor_movement = n;
}

advance_cursor()
{
        if (cursor_movement == 0)
        {
                if (update_fields(1) == 1)              /* If cursor wrapped around */
                        update_records(1);
        }
        else
                update_records(1);
}

/*
```

```
 *                   Verification Screen
 * 88/03/16  (BK)  Moved gdefs.group, current_scr initialization outside.
 */
init_menu_003 ()
{
     cls();
     directions(1); status(-1);
     draw_verification_screen();
     fields[1] = -1;
     fields[2] = -1;
     fields[3] = -1;
     switch (gdefs.pcnt)
          {
          case 1:
          case 2:
          case 3:  fields[1] = gdefs.pcnt - 1;
                   break;
          case 4:  fields[1] = 2;
                   fields[2] = 2;
                   break;
          case 5:  fields[1] = 2;
                   fields[2] = 2;
                   fields[3] = 2;
                   break;
          }
/*   gdefs.group = 0;
     group = 0;
     current_scr = 0;
*/
     return(0);
}
refresh()
{
     char buff[80];

     record = field = window = u_record = 0;
     l_record = -1;
     l_record = restore_screen(current_scr, 0);

     tot_records = get_record_count(current_scr);

     if (tot_records == 0)
     {
          add_record (new_record(), current_scr);
```

```
        redraw_record (0);
    }

    set_pfkeys(gdefs.analysis, current_scr);
    refresh_status_line();
}

refresh_status_line()
{
    char buff[BUFSIZ];

    strcpy (buff, line_message[gdefs.analysis-1]);
    if ( strcmp(gdefs.group_name[gdefs.group], "") != 0)
    {
        strcat (buff, " for ");
        strcat (buff, gdefs.group_name[gdefs.group]);
    }
    if (gdefs.analysis > 2)
        strcat (buff, (current_scr == 0) ? " before Intervention"
                                         : " after Intervention");

    message(-1, "");         /* Row 1, blinking off */
    message(-2, buff);       /* Row 2, blinking off */
}

/*-------------------------------------menu_3--------------------------------*
 *
 * 88/02/04 (BK)   Added decimal point, + sign as escapes to start
 *                 record modification.
 * 88/02/24 (BK)   Recoded F5 to call files_menu directly.
 * 88/03/16 (BK)   Moved gdefs.group, current_scr initialization inside.
 *--------------------------------------------------------------------------*/

menu_3()
{
    int     c, cnt,i;
    int     ret_val;
    /*      Records range from row 5 - row 23 */
    int     page, REFRESH = 0;
    char    buff[80];

    /* Clear the screens if data not defined */
    if ( !get_flag(D_EXIST) )
    { release_screen(0); release_screen(1); }

    init_menu_003(); gdefs.group = group = current_scr = 0;
    refresh();
```

```
ret_val = -1;

while (ret_val < 0)
    {
    /* Display the highlight bar */
    show_record_numbers();
    inverse_bar(window, field, record, clr[5]);
    c = t_getkey();
    /* Remove the bar */
    inverse_bar(window, field, record, clr[0]);
    if (REFRESH)
        {
        refresh_status_line();
        REFRESH = 0;
        }
    switch (c)
        {
        case C_LEFT : /* Move to the left */
            update_fields(-1);
            break;

        case C_RIGHT: /* Move to the right */
            update_fields(1);
            break;

        case C_UP   : /* Move up */
            update_records(-1);
            continue;
            break;

        case C_DOWN : /* Move down */
            update_records(1);
            continue;
            break;

        case HOME   : /* Go to the first record on the screen */
            record = u_record;
            break;

        case END    : /* Go to the last record on the screen */
            record = l_record;
            break;

        case F_1    : help(4,0);                   /* Pop Up Help Window */
            continue;
            break;

        case F_2    : /* Before / After */
            if (gdefs.analysis > 2)
```

```
                 before_after();
                 break;
case F_3    : /* Change Groups */
                 if (gdefs.analysis == 4)
                     change_groups();
                 break;
case F_4    : delete_record (current_scr);
                 break;
case F_5    : if (files_menu() == 1)
                 {
                     init_menu_003();
                     gdefs.group = group = current_scr = 0;
                     logo(0);
                     refresh();
                     update_parameter_window();
                 }
                 break;
case F_6    : sort_records();
                 REFRESH = 1;
                 break;
case F_7    : dine_menu(current_scr, record);
                 break;
case F_8    : if (options_menu(current_scr, record) == 1)
                 {
                     init_menu_003();
                     logo(0);
                     refresh();
                     update_parameter_window();
                 }
                 break;
case F_9    : change_directory();
                 REFRESH = 1;
                 break;
case CR     : if (modify (current_scr) == 1)
                     advance_cursor();
                 REFRESH = 1;
                 break;
case ESC    : ret_val = ESC;
                 break;
case F_10   : ret_val = 0;
                 continue;
                 break;
default     : if (window == 0 && field == 0)
                 break;
                 if ( c > 0 && isalnum(c) || c == '-'
                     || c == '+' || c == '.')
```

```
                t_ungetkey(c);
            else
                break;
            switch (modify(current_scr))
            {
                case 0: t_getkey();
                    break;
                case 1: advance_cursor();
                    break;
            }
            REFRESH = 1;
            break;
        /* switch ( t_getkey() ) */

    }       /* while (cont) */
    remove_blank_records(0);
    if (gdefs.analysis > 2)   remove_blank_records(1);
    if (records_exist())
        set_flag(D_EXIST);
    else
        clear_flag(D_EXIST);
    return(ret_val);
}

/*
 * Redisplay at most 16 records on the screen starting from
 * a specific record.
 */
restore_screen(screen, record)
int screen, record;
{
    RECORD *ptr;
    int    limit;

    scroll_fields_up (FR, LR, 0);           /* Clear the entire area */
    ptr = get_record(screen, record);      /* Retrieve the first record */
    u_record = record;
    limit = record + Max_Record; /* 17 */

    clear_parameter_fields();
    refresh_param_titles();

    while (ptr != NULL && record < limit )
    {
```

```c
        refresh_rec(get_row(record), ptr);
        ptr = ptr->next;
        record++;
    }
    return(record-1);
}

redraw_record(record)
int record;
{
    RECORD *ptr;

    /* Exit if record is not visible */
    if (record > l_record || record < u_record)
        return;

    ptr = get_record (current_scr, record);
    if (ptr == NULL)
        return;

    refresh_rec(get_row(record), ptr);
}

/* 88/03/09 (BK)  Weight not in [0,999] range output as ####. */
refresh_rec(row, ptr)
RECORD *ptr;
int row;
{
    char   buff[10];
    int    i;
    int    page = 0;
    int    win;

    /* Clear out all data */
    scroll_fields_up (row, row, 0);
    /* Output the date of analysis in  screen 11 */
    b_move  (row, locx_y[0][1], page);
    if (strcmp (ptr->date, "") == 0)
        b_writes ("          ", clr[0], page);
    else
        b_writes (ptr->date, clr[0], page);

    /* Output the number of days in file in  screen 12 */
    b_move  (row, locx_y[1][1], page);
    if (ptr->days_in_file == 0)
```

```c
        b_writes ("████████", clr[0], page);
    else
        b_writes ( itoa(ptr->days_in_file, buff, 10), clr[0], page);

    /* Output the weight in  screen 13 */
    b_move   (row, locx_y[2][1], page);
    if (ptr->actual[WEIGHT] == Unknown || ptr->actual[WEIGHT] < 0.
        || ptr->actual[WEIGHT] >= 1000.)
        b_writes ("████", clr[0], page);
    else
        b_writes (itoa ((int) ptr->actual[WEIGHT], buff, 10), clr[0], page);

    /* Output the filename  in  screen 14 */
    b_move   (row, locx_y[3][1], page);
    if (ptr->filename[0] == '\0')
        b_writes ("PUSH ENTER ", clr[0], page);
    else
        b_writes ( ptr->filename, clr[0], page);

    /* Output the day to use in analysis in  screen 15 */
    b_move   (row, locx_y[4][1], page);
    if (ptr->day_to use == 0)
        b_writes ("████████", clr[0], page);
    else
        b_writes (itoa (ptr->day_to_use, buff, 10), clr[0], page);

    /* Output the parameter values */
    refresh_param(row, ptr);
}

/*
 *  Redisplay the parameter values
 */
update_parameter_window ()
{
    RECORD  *ptr;
    int     rec;
    int     i;
    char    buff[10];
    int     page = 0;

    clear_parameter_fields();
    refresh_param_titles();
    rec = u_record;
```

```
        ptr = get_record (current_scr, rec);

        while (rec <= l_record && ptr != NULL)
            {
            refresh_param(get_row(rec), ptr);
            ptr = ptr->next;
            rec++;
            }
        }

refresh_param(row, ptr)
int row;
RECORD *ptr;
{
    int i, win, c;
    char buff[12];
    float pvalue;

    if (window == 0)
        win = 1;
    else
        win = window;

    for (i=0; i <= fields[win]; i++)
        {
        pvalue = ptr->actual[FPM+win+i-1];
        b_move   ( row, locate[i], 0);
        strcpy (buff, "██████████████");
        if (pvalue != Unknown)
            {
            switch (params[win-1+i].ptype)
                {
                case 1:  sprintf(buff, "%7.2f",pvalue);
                         break;

                case 2:
                case 3:
                case 4:
                case 5:  c = (int) pvalue;
                         if (c < 1) warning("Pvalue error");
                         else
                         sprintf(buff,"%10s",params[win-1+i].cname[c-1]);
                         break;
                }
            }
        }
}
```

```
        b_writes (buff, clr[0], 0);
    }
}

refresh_param_titles()
{
int i, win;

if (window == 0)
    win = 1;
else
    win = window;

for (i=0; i <= fields[win]; i++)
    {
    b_centers(params[win-1+i].pname, FR-3, locate[i], locate[i]+10, clr[0], 0);
    if (params[win-1+i].ptype > 1)
        b_centers("Category", FR-2, locate[i], locate[i]+10, clr[0], 0);
    else
        b_centers("        ", FR-2, locate[i], locate[i]+10, clr[0], 0);
    }
}

add_record(ptr, s)
RECORD *ptr;
int s;
{
    set_flag(D_MODIFY);
    add_link (ptr,s);
    tot_records++;
    if (get_row(l_record) < LR)
        l_record++;
    return(tot_records);
}

update_records (direction)
int direction;
{

RECORD *ptr;

record += direction;

if (record == 50)
    {
```

```
    warning("Maximum number of records reached");
    record -= 1;
    return(-1);
}

if (record == tot_records)
{
    ptr = get_record (current_scr, tot_records-1);
    if (ptr->day_to_use != 0)
    {
        add_record (new_record(), current_scr);
        redraw_record (tot_records-1);
    }
}

if (record < 0 || record >= tot_records)
{
    record -= direction;
    return(-1);
}

/* Scroll up */
if (get_row(record) > LR)
{
    l_record++;
    if (l_record < tot_records)
    {
        u_record++;
        scroll_fields up(FR, LR, 1);
        redraw_record (l_record);
    }
    else
        l_record--;
}

/* Scroll down */
else
if (get_row(record) < FR)
{
    u_record--;
    if (u_record >= 0)
    {
        if (get_row(l_record) > LR) l_record--;
        scroll_fields_down(FR, LR, 1);
        redraw_record ( u_record);
```

```
        }
    else
        u_record++;
    }
    return(0);
}

scroll_fields_up(start, finish, num)
int start;
int finish;
int num;
{
    int f;
    for (f=0;f < 8;f++)
        b_scrollup(start, locx_y[f][1], finish,
            locx_y[f][1] + sizex_y[f][1] - 1 , num, clr[0]);
}

clear_parameter_fields()
{
    int f;

    for (f=0; f< 3; f++)
    {
        b_scrollup(FR, locate[f], LR, locate[f]+9, 0, clr[0]);
        b_scrollup(FR-3, locate[f],  FR-3, locate[f]+9, 0, clr[0]);
    }
}

scroll_fields_down(start, finish, num)
int start;
int finish;
int num;
{
    int f;
    for (f=0;f < 8;f++)
        b_scrolldown(start, locx_y[f][1], finish,
            locx_y[f][1] + sizex_y[f][1] - 1 , num, clr[0]);
}

/*
* Move to the new field and possible put up a new parameter window
* return 1 - wraped around
*         0 - otherwise
*/
```

```
update_fields(direction)
int direction;
{
    int ret_val;
    field += direction;
    ret_val = 0; /* OK */

    /* Scroll left, jump into the window to the left */
    if (field < 0)
    {
        window -= 1;

        switch (window)
        {

        case -1 : window = 0;
                  field  = 0;
                  break;

        case  0 : field = fields[window];
                  break;

        case  1 :
        case  2 : field = 0;
                  if (gdefs.pcnt > 3)
                      update_parameter_window();
                  break;

        }

    }

    /* If moving right ==> into a new window */
    if (field > fields[window])
    {
        window += 1;

        /* Wrap right around from last window */
        if (window > 3 || fields[window] < 0)
        {
            window = 0;
            ret_val = 1;              /* Wraped around */
        }

        if (window > 1 )
            field = fields[window];
        else
            field = 0;

        if (gdefs.pcnt > 3)
```

```
        update_parameter_window();
    }
    return(ret_val);
}

/*
 * Delete either a record or a field
 */
delete_record (s)
int s;
{   int    i, ok;
    RECORD *rec_ptr;

    help_on (4, 1);
    ok = prompt(0,1, -3, "Delete record (Y/N)?", NULL, 0);
    help_off();

    if (ok)
    {
        if ( get_record_count(s) > 0)
            rec_ptr = get_record(s, record);
        else
            return(-1);
        if ( remove_link(rec_ptr, s, gdefs.group) != NULL)
        {
            tot_records--;
            scroll_fields_up(get_row(record), LR, 1);
            if (l_record == tot_records)
                l_record--;
            redraw_record (l_record);
            if (record > l_record)
                record--;
            set_flag(D_MODIFY);
        }
        if ( tot_records == 0)
        {
            record=0;
            add_record (new_record(), current_scr);
            redraw_record (0);
            set_flag(D_MODIFY);
        }
    }
```

```c
sort_records ()
{
    int     i,choice;

    i = 0;
    help_on (4, 2);
    choice = prompt(2, 1, -3,"Sort by date ascending or descending (A/D)?");
    help_off();
    if (choice == 'a' || choice == 'A')
    {
        remove_blank_records(current_scr);
        sort_by_date (current_scr, gdefs.group, 1);
        i = 1;
    }
    else
    if (choice == 'd' || choice == 'D')
    {
        remove_blank_records(current_scr);
        sort_by_date (current_scr, gdefs.group, -1);
        i = 1;
    }

    if (i == 1)
    {
        init_menu_003();
        refresh();
        update_parameter_window();
        set_flag(D_MODIFY);
    }
}

/*
 * Modify the field in the record in the current screen
 *
 * Return 0 - if no user input accepted
 *        1 - modify succseeful
 */
modify (s)
int s;
{
    int key, day, win, choice, c;
    char *ptr, file[13];
    RECORD *rec_ptr;
    float   fval;
    int     p, category, ret_val;
    long    lval;
```

```c
ret_val = -1;

rec_ptr = get_record(s, record);
if (window == 0)
{
    switch (field)
    {
        case 0 :
            ptr = select_data_file (file, &key, &day);
            if (key == CR && ptr != NULL)
                perform_file_loading(s, ptr, day, rec_ptr);
            break;
        case 1 : /* Get the day of analysis to use from this file */
            if (rec_ptr->days_in_file == 0)
            {
                message(2, "SELECT DATA FILE FIRST");
                return(0);
                break;
            }
            save_cursor();
            show_cursor();
            help_on(4,3);
            default_keys();
            c = wgetl(&lval, get_row(record), locx_y[4][1],
                      sizex_y[4][1], clr[0]);
            help_off();
            restore_cursor();
            if (c == CR)
            { /* Check the range of the answer */
                if (lval > 0L && lval <= (long) rec_ptr->days_in_file)
                {
                    rec_ptr->day_to_use = (int) lval;
                    c = quick_load (rec_ptr->filename, (int) lval, rec_ptr);
                    if (c < 0)
                    {
                        process_error(c, 1);    /* Use blinking message */
                    else
                    {
                        refresh_status_line();
                        ret_val = 1;
                    }
                }
                else
                    message(2, "VALID DAY IS 1 - %d ONLY", rec_ptr->days_in_file);
```

```c
            }
         break;
      }
   }
else
   {
   if (rec_ptr->day_to_use != 0)
      {
      p = window - 1 + field;
      if (params[p].ptype == 1)
         {
         save_cursor();
         show_cursor();
         help_on(4,8);
         default_keys();
         key = wgetf(&fval, get_row(record), locate[field], 10, clr[0]);
         help_off();
         restore_cursor();
         if (key == CR)
            {
            if ( fval < Min || fval > Max )
               warning("Must be %.1f to %+.1f", Min, Max);
            else
               {
               rec_ptr->actual[FPM+p] = fval;
               ret_val = 1;
               }
            }
         }
      else
         {
         if (t_keywait())            /* If a key is pending */
            {
            c = t_getkey();
            category = c - (int) '0';
            if (category >= 1 && category <= params[p].ptype)
               {
               rec_ptr->actual[FPM+p] = (float) category;
               ret_val = 1;
               }
            else
               {
               message(2,"Use keys 1 thru %d to select a category for %s",
                  params[p].ptype, params[p].pname);
               return(-1);
               }
            }
```

```c
        else
        {
            c = category_menu(p);
            if (c >= 1 && c <= params[p].ptype)
            {
                rec_ptr->actual[FPM+p] = (float) c;
                ret_val = 1;
            }
            else
                return(-1);
        }
    }
}
else
{
    if (rec_ptr->filename[0] == '\0')
        message(2,"SELECT DATA FILE AND DAY TO USE FIRST");
    else
        message(2,"SELECT DAY TO USE FIRST");
    return(0);
}

redraw_record(record);
set_flag(D_MODIFY);
return(ret_val);
}

/* Load single or multiple data files into the verification screen */
perform_file_loading(s, ptr, day, rec_ptr)
char *ptr; RECORD *rec_ptr;
int s;      /* Screen */
int day;    /* Day value */
{
    int day_to_load, c, d;

    for (d=0; d<7; d++)
    {
        if (day < 0) /* Perform multiple file loading */
        {
            if ( ( (-1 * day) & (1 << d)) != 0 )
                day_to_load = d+1;
            else
                day_to_load = 0;
            if (day_to_load == 0) continue;
```

```c
            rec_ptr = get_record(s, record);
        }
        else
        { day_to_load = day; d = 6; }

        if ( (c = quick_load (ptr, day_to_load, rec_ptr)) >= 0)
        {
            set_flag(D_MODIFY);
            refresh_status_line();
            redraw_record(record);
            if (update_records (1) == -1)
                return;
        }
        else
        {
            refresh_status_line();
            process_error(c, 1);
        }
    } /* for (d=0; d<7; d++) */
}

/*
* Mode    0 -> Normalize the bar
*         1 -> Invert the bar
*/

inverse_bar (window, field, record, attr)
int window, field, record; char attr;
{
    int page = 0;

    if (window == 0)                        /* Non parameter fields */
    {
        b_move (get_row(record), locx_y[3+field][1], page);
        b_inverse (sizex_y[3+field][1], attr, page, 0);
    }
    else                                    /* Highlight a parameter field */
    {
        b_move (get_row(record), locate[field], page);
        b_inverse (sizex_y[5+field][1], attr, page, 0);
    }
}

show_record_numbers ()
```

```
{
    char buff[3];
    int rec;

    b_scrollup (FR, 0, LR, 1, 0, clr[0]);
    for (rec = u_record; rec <= l_record; rec++)
    {
        b_move (get_row(rec), 0, 0);
        b_writes (itoa (rec+1, buff, 10), clr[0], 0);
    }
}

/*
*           Create the verification screen heading
*/
draw_verification_screen()
{
    draw_heading();
    draw_column_bars();
    draw_bottom_line(Max_Record);
}

draw_heading()
{
    b_move (FR-4, FC + 1, 0);
    b_writes("+-----------+-------+--------------------------------+",
    clr[0], 0);

    b_move (FR-3, FC + 1, 0);
    b_writes("|Date of | Days |     | Start |",  clr[0], 0);

    b_move (FR-2, FC + 1, 0);
    b_writes("|Analysis|in File|Wt.| File Name |   Day |",  clr[0], 0);

    b_move (FR-1, FC + 1, 0);
    b_writes("+-----------+-------+--------------------------------+",  clr[0], 0);
}

draw_column_bars()
{ int c, i;
    for(i=0; i<Max_Record; i++)
    {
        for (c=0; c<dim(vertical_bars); c++)
        {
            b_move (FR+i, FC + vertical_bars[c], 0);
            b_write('|', clr[0], 0);
        }
    }
```

```
    }

draw_bottom_line(row)
{
    b_move (FR+row, FC + 1, 0);
    b_writes("+-----------+-----------+-----------+-----------+-----------+-----------+", clr[0], 0);
}

set_pfkeys(analysis, scr)
int analysis, scr;
{

    if (analysis == 1 || analysis == 2)
        pfkeys(2);
    else
        if (analysis == 3)
            pfkeys(3 + scr);
        else
            pfkeys(5 + scr);
}

before_after()
{
    if (gdefs.analysis > 2)
    {
        if (current_scr == 0)
            current_scr = 1;
        else
            current_scr = 0;
        refresh();
    }
}

change_groups()
{
    gdefs.group++;

    if (gdefs.group == gdefs.gcnt)
        gdefs.group = 0;

    refresh();
}
```

MENU_004.C

```c
#include <stdio.h>
#include <conio.h>
#include "..\struct.h"
#include "..\extern.h"
#include "..\graph.h"

static char   plot_description[BUFSIZ];

char *
get_plot_description(void)
{
    return(plot_description);
}

static MENU    menu1[] = {
    "Graph Type Menu"           , 0,
    ""                          , -2,
    "Line Graph of Y vs Time    [1]", 1,
    "Bar Graph of Y vs Time     [2]", 2,
    "Box & Whiskers Graph of Y  [3]", 3,
    "Scatter Graph of Y vs X    [4]", 4,
    "Nutrient Breakdown by Calories [5]", 5,
    ""                          , -2,
    "Select with arrow keys"    , 0,
    "or press number"           , 0,
};

static MENU KEYS
menu_keys1[] = {
    {ESC, ESC}, {F_1, F_1},
    {'1', 1}, {'2', 2}, {'3', 3}, {'4', 4}, {'5', 5},
};

static MENU    menu2[] = {
    "Graph Type Menu"           , 0,
    ""                          , -2,
    "Box & Whiskers Graph of Y            [1]", 1,
    "Scatter Graph of Y vs X              [2]", 2,
    "Box & Whiskers Graph of Y by X Category [3]", 3,
    ""                          , -2,
    "Select with arrow keys"    , 0,
    "or press number"           , 0,
};
```

```
static MENU KEYS
menu_keys2[] = {
                {ESC, ESC}, {F_1, F_1},
                {'1', 1}, {'2', 2}, {'3', 3},
              };

static MENU    menu3[] = {
                "Graph Type Menu", 0,
                "", -2,
                "Bar Graph of Median Y Before & After  [1]", 1,
                "Box & Whiskers Graph of Y Before & After  [2]", 2,
                "Box & Whiskers Graph of  Y          [3]", 3,
                "", -2,
                "Select with arrow keys", 0,
                "or press number", 0,
              };

static MENU KEYS
menu_keys3[] = {
                {ESC, ESC}, {F_1, F_1},
                {'1', 1}, {'2', 2}, {'3', 3},
              };

static MENU    menu4[] = {
                "Graph Type Menu", 0,
                "", -2,
                "Bar Graph of Median  Y by Group   [1]", 1,
                "Box & Whiskers Graph of  Y by Group  [2]", 2,
                "", -2,
                "Select with arrow keys", 0,
                "or press number", 0,
              };

static MENU KEYS
menu_keys4[] = {
                {ESC, ESC}, {F_1, F_1},
                {'1', 1}, {'2', 2},
              };

/*
 *                Type of analysis
 *
 * 88/02/16 (BK)   Disabled F2-F5 keys after reorganizing help file.
 * 88/02/22 (BK)   Added code to save old description, restore on ESC.
 */

menu_004()
{
    int   key=0, c, ret_val = -1;
    char old_description[BUFSIZ];
```

```c
status(-1); directions(0);
pfkeys(8+gdefs.analysis);
cls();
memcpy(old_description, plot_description, BUFSIZ);
while (ret_val == -1)
    {
    switch (gdefs.analysis)
        {
    case 1: /* Individual Analysis */
        set_menu_keys(menu_keys1, dim(menu_keys1));
        c = get_menu_selection(&key, menu1, dim(menu1),
                               -1, -1, clr[0], Border);
        if (c > 0 && c < 5) strcpy (plot_description, menu1[1+c].line);
        break;
    case 2: /* Individual Analysis */
        set_menu_keys(menu_keys2, dim(menu_keys2));
        c = get_menu_selection(&key, menu2, dim(menu2),
                               -1, -1, clr[0], Border);
        if (c > 0 && c < 5) strcpy (plot_description, menu2[1+c].line);
        break;
    case 3: /* Individual Analysis */
        set_menu_keys(menu_keys3, dim(menu_keys3));
        c = get_menu_selection(&key, menu3, dim(menu3),
                               -1, -1, clr[0], Border);
        if (c > 0 && c < 5) strcpy (plot_description, menu3[1+c].line);
        break;
    case 4: /* Individual Analysis */
        set_menu_keys(menu_keys4, dim(menu_keys4));
        c = get_menu_selection(&key, menu4, dim(menu4),
                               -1, -1, clr[0], Border);
        if (c > 0 && c < 5) strcpy (plot_description, menu4[1+c].line);
        break;
        }
    switch (c)
        {
    case ESC : memcpy(plot_description, old_description, BUFSIZ);
               ret_val = ESC;
               break;
    case F_1 : help(5,gdefs.analysis-1);
               break;
    default  : gdefs.plot = c;
               c = strlen(plot_description);
               if (c > 2)
                  {
                  , plot_description[c-3] = '\0';
```

```
            strrmtb(plot_description);
        }
        ret_val = 0;
        break;
    }
}
if (ret_val == 0)
{
    if (gdefs.plot == 5)
    {
        strcpy (gdefs.graphs.unit[0][Y], "Percent");
        set_flag(G_VARIABLES);    /* Indicate that the variables were chosen */
    }
    else clear_flag(G_VARIABLES);
    return (0);
}
else
    return (ret_val);
}
```

MENU_005.C (partial listing)

```c
#include <stdlib.h>
#include <stdio.h>
#include <ctype.h>
#include <dos.h>
#include <string.h>
#include <conio.h>
#include <malloc.h>
#include "..\dinescor.h"
#include "..\struct.h"
#include "..\extern.h"

extern char *plot_description;
/*   Location in row, col for each region */
static int    offx_y[3][2] = {
                               { 1, 1 },   /* Date of analysis */
                               { 1, 3 },   /* Date of analysis */
                               { 1, 14},   /* Date of analysis */
                              };

/*   Size in number of rows, number of columns for each region */
static int    sizex_y[3][2] = {
                               { 1, 1},    /* Parameter window # 1 */
                               { 1, 10},   /* Parameter window # 1 */
                               { 1, 10},   /* Parameter window # 1 */
                              };

/* get the screen row for a logical record */
#define get_row(r) locate[0] + offx_y[0][0] + ( (r+1) * 2 )
#define get_col(f) locate[1] + offx_y[f][1]

#define Visible_Records     5

static int    locate[2] = { 2, 30};
static int    field, record;
static int    first_field, last_field;
static int    plot_type;

#define Max_Rows    6
#define Max_Cols    6
#define Size        10

static int    variables_chosen;
```

```c
static int      v_row, v_col;
static int      v_maxrow, v_maxcol;
static int      v_count;
static int      v_spacing;
static int      v_locate    = 15;
static char     array[Max_Rows][Max_Cols][Size+1] = {

{"TOTAL CAL","PROTEIN","SAT FAT","MONO FAT","POLY FAT","CMPLX CARB"},
{"DIET.FIBER","SUGAR","CHOLESTRL","SODIUM","POTASSIUM","VITAMIN A"},
{"VITAMIN C","IRON","CALCIUM","DINE SCORE","ICL","AGE"},
{"SEX","%TOTAL FAT","POLY/SAT","SODM/POTM","%PROTEIN","%SAT FAT"},
{"%MONO FAT","%POLY FAT","%COMP CARB","%SUGAR","WEIGHT", "%ALCOHOL"},
};

static char     unit[Max_Rows][Max_Cols][21] = {

{"Cal","Cal","Cal","Cal","Cal"},
{"Gm","Cal","Mg","Mg","Mg","RE"},
{"Mg","Mg","Mg","Score","Cal","Years"},
{"M/F 1/2","Percent","Ratio","Ratio","Percent","Percent"},
{"Percent","Percent","Percent","Percent","Lbs","Percent"},
};

/*
 *              Verification Screen
 */

menu_005()
{
    int     ret_val,c ;

    init_menu_005();

    ret_val = -1;

    update_fields(-1);

    while (ret_val < 0)
    {
        /* Display the highlight bar */
        invert_bar(field, record, clr[5]);
        c = t_getkey();
        /*Remove the bar */
        invert_bar(field, record, clr[0]);
```

```
switch (c)
    {
    case C_LEFT :   /* Move to the left */
                    update_fields(-1);
                    break;

    case C_RIGHT:   /* Move to the right */
                    update_fields(1);
                    break;

    case C_UP   :   /* Move up */
                    update_records(-1);
                    break;
    case C_DOWN :   /* Move down */
                    update_records(1);
                    break;

    case HOME   :   /* Go to the first record on the screen */
                    record = 0;
                    break;
    case END    :   /* Go to the last record on the screen */
                    record = 4;
                    break;
    case F_1    :   help(6,0);                /* Pop Up Help Window */
                    break;

    case CR     :   if (modify() == 0 && update_fields(1) == 1)
                        {
                        update_records(1);
                        update_fields(-1);
                        }
                    break;
    case ESC    :   ret_val = ESC;
                    break;
    case F_10   :   ret_val = 0;
                    break;
    }   /* switch ( t_getkey() ) */
    }   /* while (cont) */
close_menu_005();
if (ret_val == 0)
    {
    if (variables_chosen)
        return(0);
    else
        return(-1);
    }
```

```
else
     return(ESC);
}
```

```
MENU_006.C

#include <stdio.h>
#include <ctype.h>
#include <dos.h>
#include <string.h>
#include <conio.h>
#include <stdlib.h>
#include "..\struct.h"
#include "..\extern.h"
#include "..\dinescor.h"

#define BASE_ROW     3        /* Base row for first parameter record */
#define BASE_COL     0        /* Base col for first parameter record */
#define COLUMN      14

#define NAMES 19
#define Nsize 10
#define Usize 10
#define Dsize 6

static int     element[NAMES] =
{ Age, Sex, WEIGHT, ICL, 0 , 1, 2, 3, 4, 5, 6, 7, 8, 9, 10, 11, 12, 13, 14 };

/*
 * Type 0 = int
 * Type 1 = float
 * Type 3 = string
 */
static int     types[NAMES] =
{ 0, 3, 0, 0, 0, 0, 0, 0, 0, 0, 0, 0, 0, 0, 0, 0, 0, 0, 0};

static char    names[NAMES][Nsize+1] = {
"AGE", "SEX", "WEIGHT", "ICL", "TOTAL CAL","PROTEIN","SAT FAT","MONO FAT",
"POLY FAT", "CMPLX CARB", "DIET FIBER","SUGAR","CHOLESTRL","SODIUM","POTASSIUM",
"VITAMIN A", "VITAMIN C","IRON","CALCIUM",
};

static char    unit[NAMES][Usize+1] =
{
"Years", "",  "Lbs", "Cal", "Cal","Cal","Cal","Cal",
"Gm","Cal","Mg","Mg","Mg","RE",
"Mg","Mg","Mg",
};
```

```c
static MENU_KEYS wgets_keys[] = {
                                  {ESC, ESC},
                                  {F_10, CR},
                                };

static char    *undefined = "██████████";
static int data_changed;
static int field;
static RECORD tmp, *ptr;

/* 88/02/16  (BK)   Added +,- keys as escapes for modifying fields. */
/* 88/02/29  (BK)   Warning message if null record. */
/* 88/03/04  (BK)   Set D_MODIFY if record modified. */
/* 88/03/09  (BK)   Convert alcohol to calories. */

modify_values(scr, rec)
int scr, rec;
{

  int  c, ret_val;

  data_changed = 0;
  ptr = get_record(scr, rec);

  if (ptr->version == 0)
  { warning("Record cannot be modified");
    return (0);
  }

  /* Transfer the current parameter definitions into a temporary structure*/
  memcpy ((void *) &tmp, (void *) ptr, sizeof(RECORD));

  /* Convert alcohol from percent to calories, since calculate_dine_score
     expects calorie value. */
  tmp.actual[ALCOHOL] *= tmp.actual[0] / 100.0;

  cls();
  put_up_names();                /* Display the parameter definition grid */
  status(-1); pfkeys(13); directions(0);
  ret_val = 0;
  field = 0;
  while (ret_val == 0)
  {
    highlight (clr[5]);          /* Highlight the field */
    help_on (4, 15);
    c = t_getkey();
    help_off ();
```

```
    highlight (clr[0]);        /* remove the highlight*/
    switch (c)
      {
      case C_UP:    if (field > 0)
                       field--;
                    else
                       field = NAMES-1;
                    break;
      case C_DOWN:  if (field < NAMES-1)
                       field++;
                    else
                       field = 0;
                    break;
      case ESC :    if (data_changed)
                       {
                       message(1, "All changes will be lost");
                       if ( prompt (0, 2, -1, "Proceed (Y/N)?") )
                          ret_val = ESC;
                       message(-1, "");
                       }
                    else
                       ret_val = ESC;
                    break;
      case F_2 :    change_date();
                    break;
      case F_10:    /*    Done                   */
                    ret_val = 1;
                    break;
      case CR  :    modify();
                    break;
      default  :    if (c > 0 && (isdigit(c) || c == '+' || c == '-')
                          && element[field] != Sex)
                       {
                       t_ungetkey(c);
                       modify();
                       }
                    break;
      }

   }

if (ret_val != ESC)
   {
   /* Save the new parameter definitions */
   calculate_dine_score(&tmp);
   memcpy ((void *) ptr, (void *) &tmp, sizeof(RECORD));
```

```c
    if (data_changed) set_flag(D_MODIFY);
    }
  return(1);
}

static modify()
{
  int row, col, c;
  long lval;

  row = BASE_ROW + field;
  col = BASE_COL + COLUMN;
  set_wget_keys (wgets_keys, dim(wgets_keys) );    /* Return Keys */
  if (element[field] == Sex)
  {
  c = prompt(2, row, -1, "Male or female (M/F)?");
  switch(c)
    {
    case 'M':
    case 'm':    data_changed = 1;
                 tmp.actual[element[field]] = 1.0;
                 break;

    case 'F':
    case 'f':    data_changed = 1;
                 tmp.actual[element[field]] = 2.0;
                 break;

    }
  }
  else
    {
    save_cursor();
    show_cursor();
    help_on (4, 16);
    default_keys();
    c = wgetl(&lval, row, col, Dsize, clr[1]);
    restore_cursor();
    help_off();
    if (c == CR)
      {
    if ( (float) lval <= Max && (float) lval >= Min)

      data_changed = 1;
      tmp.actual[element[field]] = (float) lval;

    else warning("Must be %.1f to %+.1f", Min, Max);
      }
```

```
        }
    display_value(field);
}

change_date()
{
    char *date, buff[10];
    char *get_date();
    int key;

    strcpy (buff, "");
    set_wget_keys (wgets_keys, dim(wgets_keys) );   /* Return Keys */
    help_on (4, 17);
    key = prompt(1, 3, -1, "Date of analysis (MM/DD/YY):", buff, 8);
    help_off();
    if (key == CR)
    {
        date = get_date(buff);
        if (date == NULL)
            warning("Invalid date format");
        else
        {
            data_changed = 1;
            strcpy (tmp.date, date);
            put_up_header();
        }
    }
}

/*
 * Display the parameter record at logical location l
 */
static
display_value(l)
int l;
{
    int row, col, page, i; char buff[Dsize+1];

    row = BASE_ROW + 1;
    col = BASE_COL + COLUMN;
    clear_name(l);
    page = 0;

    if (tmp.actual[element[l]] == Unknown)
        strcpy (buff, undefined);
```

```
    else
        switch(types[1])
        {
        case 0 :        /* Integer */
                sprintf (buff, "%6.0f", tmp.actual[element[1]]);
                break;

        case 3 :  /* String */
                sprintf (buff, "%6s", ( tmp.actual[element[1]]  == 1.0)
                                   ? "MALE" : "FEMALE" );

                break;
        }
        b_move (row, col, page);
        b_writes(buff, clr[0], page);       /* Display the name */
}

/*
 * Clear all the fields on the given row in the grid
 */
static clear_name(l)
int l;
{
    int row, col, i;

    row = BASE_ROW + 1;
    col = BASE_COL + COLUMN;

    b_scrollup (row, col, row, col + Dsize - 1, 0, clr[0]);
}

static put_up_header()
{
    char buff[BUFSIZ];

    sprintf (buff, "Analysis for %s on %8s from file %s", tmp.individual, tmp.date,
                   tmp.filename);
    b_centers (buff, 2, 0, 79, clr[0], 0);
}

static put_up_names()
{
    int row, col, page, i;
    char buff[BUFSIZ];
```

```
page = 0;
row = BASE_ROW;
col = BASE_COL;

put_up_header();

for (i=0; i < NAMES; i++)
    {
    sprintf(buff, "%10s = [        ] %-10s", names[i], unit[i]);
    b_move(row++, col, page);
    b_writes(buff, clr[0], page);
    display_value(i);
    }

}

static
highlight(attr)
char attr;
{

int row, col;

row = BASE_ROW + field;
col = BASE_COL + COLUMN;

b_move (row, col, 0);
b_inverse (Dsize, attr, 0, 0);
}
```

RECORDS.C

```c
#include <stdlib.h>
#include <stdio.h>
#include <ctype.h>
#include <dos.h>
#include <string.h>
#include <conio.h>
#include <malloc.h>
#include "..\struct.h"
#include "..\extern.h"
#include "..\dinescor.h"

/* 88/03/23 (BK)   Clear screen before exiting. */
RECORD *
new_record()
{
    RECORD *ptr;
    int i;

    ptr = (RECORD *) malloc (sizeof (RECORD));
    if (ptr == NULL)
    {
        warning("Unable to allocate memory for data record <ABORTING>");
        cls();
        .exit(1);
    }

    ptr->next = NULL;
    ptr->prev = NULL;

    strcpy (ptr->filename, "");
    strcpy (ptr->individual, "");
    strcpy (ptr->date, "");
    ptr->day_to_use = 0;

    /* First parameter plus maximum parameters */
    clear_dine_arrays(ptr);

    ptr->days_in_file = 0;
    ptr->version = 0;

    return((RECORD *)ptr);
}
```

```c
/*
 * Release the memory used by screen
 */
release_screen (s)
int s;
{
    RECORD *next;
    RECORD *ptr;
    int group;

    for(group = 0; group < MaxGroups; group++)
    {
        ptr = vscreens[group][s] ;
        while (ptr != NULL)
        {
            next = ptr->next;
            free(ptr);
            ptr = next;
        }
        vscreens[group][s]  = NULL;
    }
    return(0);
}

RECORD *
get_record(s, record)
int s, record;
{
    RECORD *ptr;
    int    cnt;

    ptr = vscreens[gdefs.group][s] ;

    cnt = 0;

    for (cnt=0; cnt < record; cnt++)
    {
        if (ptr == NULL)
            return(NULL);
        else
            ptr = ptr->next;
    }
```

```
        return(ptr);
}

/*
 * Add a record to the verification screens linked list
 */
add_link(rec, screen)
RECORD *rec;
int screen;
{

    RECORD *ptr;
    ptr = vscreens[gdefs.group][screen];

    if (ptr == NULL)
        vscreens[gdefs.group][screen]  = rec;
    else
        {
        while (ptr->next != NULL) ptr = ptr->next;
        ptr->next = rec;
        rec->prev = ptr;
        }
        return(0);
}

/*
 * Add a record to the verification screens linked list
 */
insert_link(rec, screen)
RECORD *rec;
int screen;
{

    RECORD *ptr;
    ptr = vscreens[gdefs.group][screen] ;

    if (ptr == NULL)
        vscreens[gdefs.group][screen]  = rec;
    else
        {
        while (ptr->next != NULL) ptr = ptr->next;
        ptr->next = rec;
        rec->prev = ptr;
        }
        return(0);
}
```

```c
/*
 * Return the total number of records in the screen
 */
get_record_count(screen)
int screen;
{
    int count;
    RECORD *ptr;

    count = 0;
    ptr = vscreens[gdefs.group][screen] ;
    while (ptr != NULL)
    {
        count++;
        ptr = ptr->next;
    }
    return(count);
}

RECORD *
remove_link (ptr, s, group)
RECORD *ptr;
int s, group;
{
    RECORD *next, *prev;

    if (ptr == NULL)
        return(NULL);

    next = ptr->next;
    prev = ptr->prev;

    if (prev == NULL)
    {
        next->prev = NULL;
        vscreens[group][s]  = next;
    }
    else
    {
        prev->next = next;
        if (next != NULL)
            next->prev = prev;
```

```c
        }
        free(ptr);
        return(ptr);
}

remove_blank_records(screen)
int screen;
{
    RECORD *ptr;
    int group;

    for (group = 0; group < gdefs.gcnt; group++)
    {
        ptr = vscreens[group][screen];
        while (ptr != NULL)
        {
            if (ptr->day_to_use == 0)
            {
                remove_link (ptr, screen, group);
            }
            ptr = ptr->next;
        }
    }
    return(0);
}

/* 88/03/04 (BK)  Replaced gdefs.analysis error message with return. */
records_exist()
{
    int ok, s, group, n;
    RECORD *ptr;

    ok = FALSE;

    if (gdefs.analysis > 4 || gdefs.analysis < 0)  return(FALSE);
    n = (gdefs.analysis > 2) ? 2 : 1;
    for (s=0; s < n; s++)
    {
        for (group = 0; group < gdefs.gcnt && !ok; group++)
        {
            ptr = vscreens[group][s];
            if (ptr != NULL && ptr->day_to_use > 0)
            {
                ok = TRUE;
```

```
            }
        }
    }
    return(ok);
}
```

STATS.C

```c
#include <stdio.h>
#include <stdlib.h>
#include <search.h>
#include "..\struct.h"
#include "..\extern.h"
#include "..\dinescor.h"
#include "..\graph.h"

static struct scores    {  float val, rank;
                           int sample;
                         } data[250];

static struct scores  *data_ptr[250];

static float   x_val[50];
static float   y_val[50];

extern int diff(struct scores * *arg1, struct scores * *arg2);
extern int diff_abs(struct scores * *arg1, struct scores * *arg2);

/*------------------------------------------Spearman-----------------------------------*
 * Calculates Spearman rank correlation coefficient.
 * (1) Rank X and Y data by value.
 * (2) Calculate differences in ranks (di values).
 * (3) Return 1 - 6 sum(di**2) / (N**3 - N).
 * Assumes X, Y variables have same number of values, at most 50.
 *
 * 88/03/23 (BK)  Corrected calculation of N**3 (done as float).
 *-------------------------------------------------------------------------------------*/

float Spearman()
{
   int N, i; float di, sum, rs;

   N = npoints[X];             /* N equals the number of values */

   if ( N < 1) return ((float) -1.0);

   /* Load the data for the x observance */
   for (i=0; i < N; i++)
     {
       data[i].val = dvalue[X][i];
```

```c
        data_ptr[i]    = &data[i];
    }
    rank_data (N, diff);        /* Rank the data */
    for (i=0; i < N; i++) x_val[i] = data[i].rank;

    /* Load the data for the y observance */
    for (i=0; i < N; i++)
    {
        data[i].val = dvalue[Y][i];
        data_ptr[i]    = &data[i];
    }
    rank_data (N, diff);        /* Rank the data */
    for (i=0; i < N; i++) y_val[i] = data[i].rank;

    /* Get the summation of di squared */
    sum = 0.0;
    for (i=0; i < N; i++)
    {
        di = x_val[i] - y_val[i];
        sum += (di * di);
    }

    rs = 1.0 - ( (6.0 * sum) / ((float) N * (float) (N * N) - (float) N) ) ;

    return((float)rs);
}

/*----------------------------Wilcoxon----------------------------*
 * Calculates Wilcoxon matched-pairs signed-rank test statistic.
 * (1) Rank differences in pairs by magnitude.
 * (2) Restore signs to ranks.
 * (3) Returns smaller sum of like-signed ranks.
 * Assumes X, Y variables have equal number of values, at most 250.
 *
 * 88/02/08 (BK)   Corrected sign restoration.
 * 88/02/29 (BK)   Added code to ignore zero differences, return N.
 *----------------------------------------------------------------*/

float Wilcoxon(int *N)
{
    int i, j;
    float di, tplus, tminus;

    /* Get differences in the pairs, ignoring zero differences. */
    for (i = 0, j = 0; i < npoints[X]; i++)
    { data[j].val = dvalue[X][i] - dvalue[Y][i];
```

```
      if (data[j].val != 0.0) data_ptr[j++] = &data[j];
  }
*N = j;
if (j < 1) return (0.0);

/* Rank data by magnitude, removing ties. */
rank_data (j, diff_abs);

/* Get sums of ranks corresponding to positive, negative differences. */
tplus = tminus = 0.0;
for (i = 0; i < j; i++)
{ if (data[i].val > 0.0)  tplus += data[i].rank;
  if (data[i].val < 0.0)  tminus += data[i].rank;
}

/* Return smaller sum. */
return((float) min (tminus, tplus));
}

/*------------------------------Kruskal Wallis------------------------------*
 * Calculates Kruskal-Wallis test statistic.
 *
 * 88/02/29 (BK)   Removed code which computed absolute values.
 *--------------------------------------------------------------------------*/
float Kruskal Wallis(Dj, Nj)
float Dj[5][50];
int Nj[5];
{
int i, k, N;
float sum, Rj[5], A, B, C, H;

/* Load the data into a local structure */
N = 0;
for (k=0; k<5; k++)
  for (i=0; i < Nj[k]; i++)
  {
    data[N].val = Dj[k][i];
    data[N].sample = k;
    data_ptr[N] = &data[N];
    N++;
  }

rank_data (N, diff);              /* Rank the data */

/* Get the summation of all the ranks */
```

```c
    for(k=0; k<5; k++)
    {
        Rj[k] = 0.0;
        for (i=0; i < N; i++)
        {
            if (data[i].sample == k)  Rj[k] += data[i].rank;
        }
    }

    sum = 0.0;
    for(k=0; k<5; k++)
    {
        if (Nj[k] > 0)
            sum += (float) ( (Rj[k] * Rj[k])/ (float) Nj[k]);
    }

    A = (float) ((float) 12 / (float) (N * (N + 1)));
    B = (float) (3 * ( N + 1));
    C = sum * A;
    H = C - B;
    return((float) H);
}

/*------------------------------------rank data----------------------*
 * Ranks N data elements using supplied compare function. Removes
 * ties by averaging.
 *
 * 88/02/08 (BK)  Revised to handle ties.
 *-------------------------------------------------------------------*/
rank_data(N, compare)
int N;
int (* compare) ();

{
    int i, this, next;
    float rank;

    /* Sort the values in increasing order. */
    qsort ( (void *) data_ptr, (size_t) N, sizeof (struct scores *), compare);

    /* Rank the sorted values from 1 to N, averaging ranks of tied elements. */
    this = 0;
    while (this < N)
    {
        next = this + 1;
        while (next < N && ((* compare) (&data_ptr[this], &data_ptr[next]) == 0))
```

```
        next++;
    rank = ((float) (this + next - 1)) / 2.0 + 1.0;
    for (i = this; i < next; i++)
        data_ptr[i]->rank = rank;
    this = next;
    }
}

/*----------------------------diff----------------------------*
 * Compares values of scores pointed to by arg1 and arg2, returning
 * difference. For use in rank_data and qsort.
 *-----------------------------------------------------------*/
int diff(arg1, arg2)
struct scores **arg1, **arg2;
{
    return( (*arg1)->val - (*arg2)->val );
}

/*--------------------------diff_abs--------------------------*
 * Compares absolute values of scores pointed to by arg1 and arg2,
 * returning difference. For use in rank_data and qsort.
 *-----------------------------------------------------------*/
int diff_abs(arg1, arg2)
struct scores **arg1, **arg2;
{
    return( abs((*arg1)->val) - abs((*arg2)->val) );
}
```

VIEWPORT.C

```c
#include <stdio.h>
#include <stdlib.h>
#include "..\struct.h"
#include "..\extern.h"
#include "..\graph.h"
#include "..\dinescor.h"

/* viewport to window mapping functions */
float   WVxm[ViewPorts],
        WVxa[ViewPorts],
        WVym[ViewPorts],
        WVya[ViewPorts];

struct Limits   w[ViewPorts], v[ViewPorts];

/*----------------------------setup_y_limits----------------------------*
 * Computes mn, mx window values for data. Sets either mn or mx
 * to 0 unless mn < 0 and mx > 0. If mode == 1 then recommended
 * ranges are included in computing mn and mx.
 *
 * 88/03/09 (BK)   Changed to set up low and high limits.
 *-----------------------------------------------------------------------*/
setup_limits(int mode, int V, int RHV, int RLV, float *mn, float *mx)
{ int i;

  *mx = *mn = dvalue[V][0];
  for (i = 1; i < npoints[V]; i++)
  { *mx = max(*mx, dvalue[V][i]); *mn = min(*mn, dvalue[V][i]); }
  if (mode == 1)
  { for (i = 0; i < npoints[RHV]; i++)
      if (dvalue[RHV][i] != Unknown)
      { *mx = max(*mx, dvalue[RHV][i]); *mn = min(*mn, dvalue[RHV][i]); }
    for (i = 0; i < npoints[RLV]; i++)
      if (dvalue[RLV][i] != Unknown)
      { *mx = max(*mx, dvalue[RLV][i]); *mn = min(*mn, dvalue[RLV][i]); }
  }
  if (*mx > 0.0 && *mn > 0.0) *mn = 0.0;
  if (*mx < 0.0 && *mn < 0.0) *mx = 0.0;
}

setup_y_limits(int mode)
{ setup_limits(mode, Y, RHY, RLY, &w[0].y.min, &w[0].y.max); }
```

```
setup_x_limits(int mode)
{ setup_limits(mode, X, RHX, RLX, &w[0].x.min, &w[0].x.max); }

use_plotting_limits()
{
    set_window_viewport(0);
}

/*
 * Convert world coordinates to screen coordinates for the selected
 * viewport vp
 */
world_to_screen(int vp, float x, float y, int *sx, int *sy)
{
    if (vp >= 0 && vp < ViewPorts)
    {
        clipv (vp, &x, &y);
        *sx = (int) (WVxm[vp] * x + WVxa[vp] + (float) 0.5);
        *sy = (int) (WVym[vp] * y + WVya[vp] + (float) 0.5);
    }
}

/*
 * Clip a point in the viewport
 * 88/03/09 (BK)   Changed from screen clipping to world clipping.
 */
clipv (vp, x, y)
int vp;
float *x, *y;
{
    float maxv, minv;

    /* Clip the y value */
    maxv = max( w[vp].y.max, w[vp].y.min);
    minv = min( w[vp].y.max, w[vp].y.min);
    if (*y > maxv) *y = maxv; else if (*y < minv) *y = minv;

    /* Clip the x value */
    maxv = max( w[vp].x.max, w[vp].x.min);
    minv = min( w[vp].x.max, w[vp].x.min);
    if (*x > maxv) *x = maxv; else if (*x < minv) *x = minv;
}

/*
 ***    Set the current window coordinate system
```

```c
*
*/
set_window(int vp, float xl, float xh, float yl, float yh)
{
    if (vp >= 0 && vp < ViewPorts)
        {
        w[vp].x.min = xl;
        w[vp].x.max = xh;
        w[vp].y.min = yl;
        w[vp].y.max = yh;
        }
}

/*
***     Define the current viewport mapping to the screen
*
*/
set_viewport(vp, xl, xh, yl, yh)
int vp, xl, xh, yl, yh;
{
    if (vp >= 0 && vp < ViewPorts)
        {
        v[vp].x.min = (float) xl;
        v[vp].x.max = (float) xh;
        v[vp].y.min = (float) yl;
        v[vp].y.max = (float) yh;
        }
}

/*
*
***     Set the window to viewport mapping for viewport vp
*
*/
set_window_viewport(vp)
int vp;
{
    float xm, ym;

    xm = w[vp].x.max - w[vp].x.min;
    if (xm == 0.0)
        {
        fprintf(stderr,"\nerror: set_window_viewport xm div by 0");/*
        xm = 1.0;
```

```c
    }
    ym = w[vp].y.max - w[vp].y.min;
    if (ym == 0.0)
    {
/*      fprintf(stderr,"\nerror: set_window_viewport ym div by 0");*/
        ym = 1.0;
    }

    if (vp >= 0 && vp < ViewPorts)
    {
        WVxm[vp] = (v[vp].x.max - v[vp].x.min) / xm;
        WVxa[vp] = v[vp].x.min - w[vp].x.min * WVxm[vp];

        WVym[vp] = (v[vp].y.max - v[vp].y.min) / ym;
        WVya[vp] = v[vp].y.min - w[vp].y.min * WVym[vp];
    }
}
```

EXTERN.H

```
extern  struct    verify_    *get_record();
extern  struct    verify_    *new_record();
extern  struct    Params params[MaxParams];
extern  struct    _gdefs gdefs;
extern  struct    verify *vscreens[MaxGroups][2];
extern  char      *get_file_name();
extern  char      *select_data_file();
extern  struct    verify *remove_link();
extern  int       prompt(int, int, int, char *, ...);
extern  void message(int, ...);
extern  void warning();

extern  int cr_flag;              /* Critical error flag */
extern  struct  cr_err  device_info;

extern  FILE *fopenr(char *);
extern  FILE *fopenw(char *);
extern  FILE *fopenrb(char *);
extern  FILE *fopenwb(char *);

extern  char clr[];
extern  char gclr[];

extern  char * strdup();
extern  int       message_row[3];
extern  int       message_color[3];

extern  DISPLAY_DEV display_dev;
extern  char *strsave();
extern  char *convert_date();
extern  char *strscan();

extern  int display_title();
extern  int round(int value,int increment,int displacement);
extern  int round_range_up(int range);
extern  int round_range_up_xl(int range);
extern  int round_increment(int inc);
extern  int round_range_down(int range);
extern  int adjust_increment(int *inc,int low,int high,int range);
extern  int load_labels(int *low,int *high,int *cnt,int *labels);
extern  int load_labels_x3(int *low,int *high,int cnt,int *labels);
extern  int load_labels_xl(int *low,int *high,int cnt,int *labels,int roundup);
extern  int plot_y_axis(int *ylow,int *yhigh,char *label,int grid);
```

```
extern  int plot_x_axis1(int *xlow,int *xhigh,char *label,int grid);
extern  int plot_x_axis_special(int *xlow,int *xhigh,char *label,int grid);
extern  int plot_x_axis3(int *xlow,int *xhigh,char *label,int grid);
extern  int plot_x_axis2(int low,int high,char *label,int grid);
extern  int plot_y_special(char *label,float ylow,float yhigh,float increment,int grid);
extern  int put_box(float xl,float yh,float xh,float yl,char *str,int color);
extern  void calculate_box_n_whiskers(int var,float *high,float *low,float *median,float *lower,float *upper);
extern  void plot_box_n_whiskers(float yl,float yh,float high,float low,float median,float lower,float upper,char *label,int color);
extern  int get_median(int var,float *result);
extern  int calculate_dine_score(struct verify_ *rec);
extern  int dump_screen(void);
extern  int print_graph(void);
extern  int view(void);
extern  int init_graphics(void);
extern  int restore_graphics(void);
extern  int show_graph(int chart,int flags);
extern  int get_user_y_range(void);
extern  int get_user_x_range(void);
extern  int g_write(int c,int row,int col,int lcol,int color);
extern  int graph_message(int mess);
extern  int graph_inquire(int num);
extern  int get_string(int x,int y,char *str,char *buff,int limit);
extern  int igp_scatter_graph(int xvar,int yvar,int plot,int flags);
extern  int igp_box_graph(int var,int plot,int flags);
extern  int igp_bar_graph(int yvar,int plot,int flags);
extern  int ind_scatter_graph(int xvar,int yvar,int plot,int flags);
extern  int ind_line_graph(int yvar,int plot,int flags);
extern  int ind_box_graph(int var,int plot,int flags);
extern  int ind_bar_graph(int yvar,int plot,int flags);
extern  int ind_nutrient_breakdown(int record,int flags);
extern  int get_difference_from_recc(int nutrient,struct verify_ *ptr);
extern  int bar(float xl,float yh,float xh,float yl);
extern  int g_centers(int font,char *buff,int row,int lcol,int rcol,int dir,int color);
extern  int y_axis(int plot,int grid);
extern  int x_axis(int plot,int var,int type,int grid);
extern  int load_array(int array,int group,int screen,int var);
extern  int remove_unknown_data(int var,int flag);
extern  int delete_element(int array,int element);
extern  int compare();
extern  int sort_arrays(void);
extern  int mgp_bar_graph(int yvar,int plot,int flags);
extern  int mgp_box_special(int var,int plot,int flags);
extern  int show_reccommended_range(void);
extern  int show_labels(int low,int high);
```

```
extern int draw_line(int yvar,int color);
extern int sgp_box_graph(int var,int plot,int flags);
extern int sgp_bar_graph(int yvar,int plot,int flags);
extern int sgp_box_special(int var,int plot,int flags);
extern float Spearman(void);
extern float Wilcoxon(int *nonzero);
extern float Kruskal_Wallis(float Dj[5][50], int Nj[5]);
extern int rank_data(int N, int (* compare)());
extern int setup_y_limits(int mode);
extern int setup_x_limits(int mode);
extern int use_plotting_limits(void);
extern int world_to_screen(int vp,float x,float y,int *sx,int *sy);
extern int clipv(int vp,float *x,float *y);
extern int set_window(int vp,float xl,float xh,float yl,float yh);
extern int set_viewport(int vp,int xl,int xh,int yl,int yh);
extern int set_window_viewport(int vp);

extern int  alcohol_content (int code, float portion);

extern int set_flag (int flag);
extern int clear_flag (int flag);
extern int get_flag (int f);
extern int reset_flags(void);

extern int save_cursor(void);
extern int restore_cursor(void);
extern void show_cursor(void);
extern void hide_cursor(void);

extern char *get_plot_description(void);
```

STRUCT.H

```c
#include "window.h"
#include "keys.h"
#include "file.h"
#include "menu.h"
#include "error.h"

#define Psize            10      /* Parameter name size */
#define Cmax             5       /* Maximum number of catagories */
#define Gsize            20      /* Parameter name size */

#define FPM              30      /* First parameter element number */

#define MaxFiles         512     /* Maximum number of files */
#define FileSize         13      /* File record size in bytes NULL delimited */
#define MaxParams        5       /* Maximum number of parameters */
#define MaxGroups        5       /* Maximum number of groups */
#define TColors          6       /* Maximum number of Text Colors */
#define GColors          4       /* Maximum number of Graphics Colors */

#define directions(num)  view_line (0, num)
#define pfkeys(num)      view_line (1, num)
#define status(num)      view_line (2, num)

#define help_on(x, y)    t_set_params (x, y)
#define help_off()       t_clear()

/* Global Flags */
#define D_EXIST          1       /* Data records exist in some form */
#define D_MODIFY         2       /* Data was modified thus requiring saving */
#define D_CHOSEN         4       /* Analysis type chosen */
#define G_SELECTED       8       /* Graph selected */
#define G_VARIABLES      16      /* Graphing variables selected */
#define P_DEFINED        32      /* Graphing variables selected */

#define cls()            clear_screen(clr[0])

#define rnd(x)           (int) (x > 0.0) ? (x + 0.5) : (x - 0.5)
#define SCREENS          struct verify_
#define RECORD           struct verify_
```

```c
#define DISPLAY_DEV struct display_

#define CGA    0    /* IBM Color Graphics Adapter */
#define EGA    1    /* IBM Enhanced Graphics Adapter */
#define HGA    2    /* Hercules Graphics Adapter */
#define MGA    3    /* IBM Monochrome Display Adapter */
#define ATT    4    /* AT&T Graphics Adapter */
#define TEC    5    /* TEMCAR Graphics Adapter */

/* Global definitions and flags */
struct _gdefs  {

    char    *path[5];        /* Path definitions */
    int     menu;            /* Current menu */
    int     analysis;        /* Analysis chosen */
    int     group;
    int     pcnt;            /* Parameter count */
    int     gcnt;            /* Group Count */
    int     three_day;       /* Three day analysis */
    int     flags;           /* Program flags */
    int     plot;            /* Type of plotting selected */
    struct  {
            int     type[5][2];
            char    name[5][2][21];
            char    unit[5][2][21];
    } graphs;
    char    *group_name[MaxGroups];
};

struct display_  {
    char    ddescrip[80];
    char    pdescrip[40];
    int     device;
    struct  {
            int     mode;
            int     colors;
            int     xmax;
            int     ymax;
    } text, graphics;
    int     printer;   /* ****************************************
                        *       Printer type defined as follows
                        *
                        *       -1- No Printer
                        *       0 - Epson FX
                        *       1 - IBM or Epson LX & MX
                        *       2 - Okidata
                        *       3 - LaserJet
                        *
```

```
          /* **************************************** */
char   tclr[TColors];      /* Text Color Table */
char   gclr[GColors];      /* Graphics Color Table */
};


struct  Params {
        char pname[Psize+1];      /* Parameter Name */
        int  ptype;               /* Parameter Type
                                     -1 : Undefined
                                      0 : Non/Catagorical
                                      2..5 : Number of catagories
                                   */
        char cname[Cmax][Psize+1]; /* If ptype ==
                                       0 : Unit Name
                                       else: Catagory names
                                    */

};


/* Verification screen record */
struct verify_ {
        char filename[FileSize+1];
        char individual[31];      /* Hold individuals name */
        int  version;
        int  day_to_use;
        int  days_in_file;
        int  weight;
        float  actual[40];        /* Actual Data Values */
        float  low[40];           /* Reccommended low range */
        float  high[40];          /* Reccommended high range */
        char date[9];
        struct verify_  *next;
        struct verify_  *prev;
        };


static MENU_KEYS def_keys[] =  {  {ESC, ESC},
                                  {F_10, CR},
                                };


#define default_keys()  set_wget_keys (def_keys, dim(def_keys))
```

Index